101
TACTICS
for
SPIRITUAL
WARFARE

101
TACTICS
for
SPIRITUAL
WARFARE

JENNIFER LeCLAIRE

CHARISMA
HOUSE

101 TACTICS FOR SPIRITUAL WARFARE by Jennifer LeClaire
Published by Charisma House
Charisma Media/Charisma House Book Group
600 Rinehart Road
Lake Mary, Florida 32746
www.charismahouse.com

Visit the author's website at www.jenniferleclaire.org.

Library of Congress Cataloging-in-Publication Data:
Names: LeClaire, Jennifer (Jennifer L.), author.
Title: 101 tactics for spiritual warfare / Jennifer LeClaire.
Other titles: One hundred one tactics for spiritual warfare | One
    hundred and one tactics for spiritual warfare
Description: Lake Mary, Florida : Charisma House, 2018. | Includes
    bibliographical references and index.
Identifiers: LCCN 2018011980 (print) | LCCN 2018014636 (ebook) |
    ISBN 9781629994963 | ISBN 9781629994956 (trade paper : alk. paper)
Subjects: LCSH: Spiritual warfare--Biblical teaching.
Classification: LCC BS680.S73 (ebook) | LCC BS680.S73 L43 2018
    (print) | DDC 235/.4--dc23
LC record available at https://lccn.loc.gov/2018011980

20 21 22 23 24 — 8 7 6 5 4
Printed in the United States of America

This book is dedicated to my dear friend Vanessa Angelini. I know of no one who is fiercer in the spirit, no one with a stronger will to see the enemy's plans fall to the ground, and no one with greater dedication to the plans and purposes of God. He has used your faithful intercession during the heated combat I face to strengthen my resolve time and time again. May God bless you with every desire of your heart as you continue pursuing a revelation of His Spirit working in and through you.

CONTENTS

ACKNOWLEDGMENTS

I AM GRATEFUL FOR my friends at Charisma House who have been diligent to attack the works of darkness with this and other spiritual warfare books. It's an honor to publish with you spiritual warriors who are fierce in Christ. Thank you for your loyalty and support.

FOREWORD

Many believers are facing spiritual struggles as they attempt to advance in the things of God. Oftentimes people assume the struggle they are facing is just a natural battle, yet just beneath the surface there is something far more complex taking place. They are under a spiritual attack!

As I discussed in my book *Overcoming Spiritual Attack*, a spiritual attack is a series of events coordinated by the demonic realm in order to abort promises, shipwreck faith, oppress a believer, and stall out destiny. The Bible tells us plainly and repeatedly that the devil has various plots and schemes he uses against human beings. Many people wrongly assume that Satan is stupid, yet he has been studying the thoughts, actions, and behavior of humanity since the beginning of time. He knows how to tempt people, and he knows what kinds of attacks will distract them from their destiny.

Thank God, He has given us His Word, and when our life experience is not lining up with His promises, we know one of two things is going on: we're either out of His will or we're under spiritual attack. Of course, discerning you're under spiritual attack is one thing; fighting off the enemy of your mind, your health, your relationships, and your finances is another. Once you recognize a spiritual attack, you need to rise up in faith and authority with the right strategy, the right tactics, and the right weapons to rebuke the enemy and break its power over your life.

In the Bible we read about many weapons of our warfare, which "are not carnal, but mighty through God to the pulling down of strongholds" (2 Cor. 10:4). We read about many strategies of the Lord to defy the enemy's plans for your life. We see that God gave different strategies and tactics to different warriors at different times for different reasons. For example, David didn't fight the same way as Joshua. Paul didn't fight the same way as Gideon. Samson didn't fight the same way as Jehoshaphat. Much the same, God has a perfect battle plan for you, and His strategies and tactics always lead you into triumph.

In *101 Tactics for Spiritual Warfare* Jennifer offers biblical tools to combat every enemy attack. She helps you identify open doors and slam them shut. She exposes the subtle wiles of the wicked one and equips you to run to the battle line in the right timing with the right tactic to see swift victory.

As you read the pages of this book, know and understand Jennifer is not writing from mere theology but both a biblical perspective and vital time-tested experience. You may have read her testimony of losing everything—including her husband, her freedom, and her livelihood. That alone is an inspiring story of overcoming the enemy's work to kill, steal, and destroy her life. But those early battles were not her only ones.

Over the years I've personally seen Jennifer walk through many different types of battles and navigate warfare that causes some to grow weary and fainthearted with strength and valor. She stood in the face of battles against her health and now walks in wholeness. She tackled enemy assignments against relationships and has seen restoration. She has wrestled with the enemy over finances and released faith that led to increase.

Jennifer is known for her practical teaching blended with prophetic insight, and this book stays true to her bold yet encouraging style. You will find strength for the battle as the pages of this book infuse you with God's Word, exhort you to stand in your authority, inspire you to fight the good fight of faith, and give you confidence that victory, though it seems elusive at times, belongs to you and is assured in Christ.

—RYAN LeSTRANGE
AUTHOR, *OVERCOMING SPIRITUAL ATTACK*
FOUNDER, TRIBE NETWORK, iHub MOVEMENT

Introduction

WHAT YOU NEED *to* KNOW
ABOUT SPIRITUAL WARFARE

"I AM IN A WAR." I wrote these five words in large letters across the bottom of my wall-sized dry-erase calendar many years ago after a strong revelation that the unseen realm is raging with spiritual enemies that intend to kill, steal, and destroy my life (John 10:10).

Paul warns us in 2 Corinthians 2:11 not to be ignorant of the devil's strategies. We need to know our enemy, know our God, and know who we are in Him—but we also need to equip ourselves with revelation on how to defeat the enemy of our souls.

It starts with acknowledging what I wrote on my wall calendar: "I am in a war."

Whether you know it or not, you are in a war. The war against God's people is raging. Many are reporting increased spiritual warfare. That's because the enemy knows his time is short. An Ephesians 6:12 cohort is pulling out all the stops to keep you from advancing the kingdom with your gifts and talents.

If you ignore the devil, the warfare doesn't stop. If you focus solely on Jesus, it does not make you immune from warfare. Yes, we should absolutely be more God-focused than demon-focused. However, if Paul the apostle—a man with deep intimacy with God who received half the books of the New Testament through direct revelation and prayed in tongues more than anyone—wrestled principalities and powers, who are we to think ignoring this reality will stop demonic attacks?

Indeed, I believe one of the devil's greatest deceptions is to convince you to lay your weapons down. Make no mistake, there is no cease-fire in the spirit. You cannot lay your weapons down and think for a moment the devil will not see it as an opportune time to go in for the kill. On the contrary, you need a battle plan. You need a strategy. You need specific tactics for specific skirmishes.

Yes, Christ has all authority. He "spoiled the principalities and powers, [and] he made a show of them openly, triumphing over them in it" (Col. 2:15, JUB). But we still have to exercise our authority and use Spirit-inspired strategies to drive the devil out.

Paul told us succinctly, "We wrestle not against flesh and blood, but against principalities, against powers, against the rulers of the darkness of this world, against spiritual wickedness in high places" (Eph. 6:12, KJV). Paul paints this descriptive picture and offers a hierarchy of demonic forces so we aren't ignorant about what we're up against.

Paul also mentions the weapons of our warfare, which "are not carnal, but mighty through God to the pulling down of strongholds" (2 Cor. 10:4). The apostle did this to help arm us for the fight.

Paul tells his spiritual son Timothy to be a good soldier (2 Tim. 2:3) and to "war a good warfare" (1 Tim. 1:18, KJV). Paul also told us not to give place to the devil (Eph. 4:27) and warned about the "snare of the devil" (1 Tim. 3:7; 2 Tim. 2:26).

Then we have James, who told us, "Submit yourselves to God. Resist the devil, and he will flee from you" (James 4:7). And Peter warned us to be sober and vigilant, because "your adversary the devil, as a roaring lion, walketh about, seeking whom he may devour" (1 Pet. 5:8, KJV). Peter told us to resist him, standing firm in the faith (v. 9). Paul also told us, "Fight the good fight of faith" (1 Tim. 6:12).

Should we ignore all these warnings and instructions? God forbid.

All these scriptures suggest that the devil is still wreaking havoc on the earth. Havoc on the earth—sickness, disease, murders, immorality, and the like—is not God's will. Jesus spoiled the principalities and powers. But the word *spoiled* doesn't mean "neutered and made powerless." Jesus plundered the kingdom of darkness. The kingdom of darkness and all the principalities and powers that call it home lost authority over the born-again believer. But we still have to enforce the kingdom rule of law on earth.

In the pages of this book you'll find 101 tactics to engage the enemy from an offensive posture and send him fleeing. Some of these tactics will be reminders. Others may be new to you. Look at this book as a warfare manual and refer to it often. In times of heavy assault, it can be hard to remember what you know. I pray the Holy Spirit uses this book to teach you, to train you, and to remind you of your victory in Christ against any and all demon powers.

SPEAK *the* NAME *of* JESUS

W HEN WE MEET with spiritual warfare, we may be tempted to wrestle the enemy in the flesh. But since we wrestle not against flesh and blood—our fight is against principalities, powers, rulers of the darkness of the age, and spiritual wickedness in high places, according to Ephesians 6:12—we won't find victory in battle by taking on enemies with our intellect, reasoning, or sheer willpower. Paul told us the weapons of our warfare are not carnal, but they are mighty in God (2 Cor. 10:4).

The mighty weapons with which God has furnished us work with one condition. We must wield this spiritual artillery under the lordship of Jesus Christ and with the authority He has given us in His name. Our baseline in any battle is understanding the power in the name of Jesus, praying in the name of Jesus, and otherwise taking authority over our enemies—which are also His enemies—in the name of Jesus.

Consider the power in the name of Jesus as Paul describes it in Philippians 2:9–11: "Therefore God highly exalted Him and gave Him the name which is above every name, that at the name of Jesus every knee should bow, of those in heaven and on earth and under the earth, and every tongue should confess that Jesus Christ is Lord, to the glory of God the Father." And again, Paul wrote: "For it is written: 'As I live, says the Lord, every knee shall bow to Me, and every tongue shall confess to God'" (Rom. 14:11).

Just like there is no other name under heaven by which we can be saved (Acts 4:12), there is no other name under heaven by which we can take authority over demon powers. In our own authority we have no ability to stand against the devil. We cannot go toe-to-toe with the devil in our flesh, nor can we effectively use His name in demonic confrontations without a revelation of the power it carries.

Jesus sent out seventy disciples two by two into territories He was about to enter. When they completed their mission, they came back with a good report: "The seventy returned with joy, saying, 'Lord, even the demons are subject to us through Your name'" (Luke 10:17). We don't know if the sons of Sceva had heard of the successes of the seventy on the mission field, but what we do know is they stepped out in the name of Jesus without a revelation of the power in His name and were met with much different results. Let's listen in to the account in Acts 19:13–17:

> Some of the itinerant Jewish exorcists invoked the name of the Lord Jesus over those who had evil spirits, saying, "We command you to come out in the name of Jesus whom Paul preaches." There were seven sons of a Jewish high priest named Sceva doing this. The evil spirit answered and said, "I know Jesus, and I know Paul, but who are you?" Then the man in whom the evil spirit was jumped on them, overpowered them, and prevailed against them, so that they fled from that house naked and wounded. This became known to all Jews and Greeks living in Ephesus. And fear fell on them all, and the name of the Lord Jesus was magnified.

Meditate on the power in the name of Jesus. Get a revelation of the power in that name before you enter into battle to exercise your authority in Christ and you will see victory.

BIND *the* HAND
of the ENEMY

IT IS NOT difficult to discern the enemy's handiwork in your life. The enemy has a threefold ministry: to kill, steal, and destroy (John 10:10). That's his vision statement, mission statement, self-appointed purpose, and goal—and it runs exactly opposite of Jesus's promise in that same verse to give you an abundant life overflowing with blessings.

Thankfully Jesus gave us the keys to the kingdom. We find this supernatural handoff in Matthew 16:19: "I will give you the keys of the kingdom of heaven, and whatever you bind on earth shall be bound in heaven, and whatever you loose on earth shall be loosed in heaven." The Amplified Classic translation gives us more insight into how to use these keys successfully in spiritual warfare: "I will give you the keys of the kingdom of heaven; and whatever you bind (declare to be improper and unlawful) on earth must be what is already bound in heaven; and whatever you loose (declare lawful) on earth must be what is already loosed in heaven."

We are not using the keys to the kingdom, then, to open a door only God can open or unlock a blessing we lust after—but to enforce God's will in the earth. It is not God's will for the enemy to steal, kill, and destroy our finances, our health, our family, or anything else He's put in our hands. Therefore, when I sense the enemy's hand meddling in my life or the life of someone I love, I use the keys of the kingdom of heaven to bind up the enemy's agenda. I bind the hand of the enemy! I slam the door in his face and lock it.

When Jesus gave you His name and the keys to His kingdom,

He gave you authority—but you have to use it. The kingdom keys bind. But it's not good enough to have the keys on a chain in your purse or hanging from your belt buckle. You can't open a door without inserting and turning the key. Jesus has done His part; He's given you the keys. Now you have to do your part; you have to turn the key. You turn the key by speaking forth the will of God out of your mouth where the enemy is concerned.

Practically speaking, if I discern the enemy is trying to steal my money, I bind the hand of the thief. If I discern the enemy trying to meddle in my relationships, I bind the hand of the destroyer. If I discern the enemy is trying to bring sickness to my doorstep, I bind the hand of infirmity demons. I say, "Devil, I bind you in Jesus's name. I bind the hand of the thief in every area of my life."

Now, after you bind the hand of the thief, be sure to loose the will of the Lord. Never bind without loosing. By loosing the will of the Lord, you are effectively declaring His kingdom is coming into that situation. So, if the enemy is trying to steal your money, you pray this way: "I bind the hand of the thief in Jesus's name over my finances, and I loose the blessing of the Lord, which makes me rich without sorrow. I loose God's harvest in my life in the name of Jesus."

Spiritual Warfare Tactic 3

LOOSE GOD'S WARRING ANGELS

Angels are real, and they are all around us. With regard to angels, Hebrews 1:14 tells us assuredly, "Are they not all ministering spirits sent out to minister to those who will inherit salvation?" If you are saved, you will inherit salvation.

We know there are warrior angels in Scripture. Second Kings 19:35 reveals, "On that night the angel of the Lord went out and struck one hundred eighty-five thousand in the camp of the Assyrians. When others woke up early in the morning, these were all dead bodies." We also know the archangel Michael fought with the prince of Persia to help another angel deliver prayer answers to Daniel (Dan. 10:13).

In the Book of Revelation we read about an epic war between good and evil—a battle between the archangel Michael and his company of holy angels and a cohort of demons. The dramatic account is recorded in Revelation 12:7–9, demonstrating the warring nature of some angels on assignment.

Jesus Himself mentioned angels in the context of war on the night of His betrayal in the Garden of Gethsemane. Peter's first response to the soldiers trying to take Jesus into custody was to pull out his sword and fight. But Jesus corrected him in Matthew 26:52–54:

> Then Jesus said to him, "Put your sword back in its place. For all those who take up the sword will perish by the sword. Do you think that I cannot now pray to My Father, and He will at once give Me more than twelve legions of

angels? But how then would the Scriptures be fulfilled, that it must be so?"

And David was utterly dependent on the Lord, but in Psalm 35:1–5 we see him call on God to send warring angels:

> Plead my cause, O Lord, with my adversaries; fight those who fight me. Take hold of the large shield and small shield, and rise up for my help. Draw the spear and javelin against those who pursue me. Say to my soul, "I am Your salvation." May those who seek my life be ashamed and humiliated; may those who plan my injury be turned back and put to shame. May they be as chaff before the wind, and may the angel of the Lord cast them down.

We do not command angels, but His Spirit can lead us to loose them or to petition Jesus, who is the Head of the angels, to release them to war on our behalf. When we confess the Word of God or make Spirit-led decrees, it also opens the realm of possibility to see angels activated to war on our behalf.

Psalm 103:20–21 reveals this reality: "Bless the Lord, you His angels, who are mighty, and do His commands, and obey the voice of His word. Bless the Lord, all you His hosts; you servants who do His pleasure." I believe when we speak the Word of God, angels' ears perk up. I believe when we make decrees by the Spirit of God, it sends angels on assignment. We don't want to fall into a rote prayer in which we're always asking God to send angels to war, because that can tie His hands. We want to give God liberty to intervene however He chooses, whether it's releasing warring angels or some other strategy from heaven. But rest assured, angels are standing by.

PRAISE
the LORD

W HEN YOU'RE IN the midst of heavy warfare, the last thing you feel like doing is praising the Lord. That's what the enemy is betting on. It seems counterintuitive to the natural mind to praise God when the devil is bombarding you with fiery darts, but it's a proven and effective spiritual warfare tactic.

The Bible says we enter His courts with praise (Ps. 100:4). The Bible says in His presence there is fullness of joy (Ps. 16:11). The Bible says the joy of the Lord is our strength (Neh. 8:10). The enemy knows if you can get in the presence of God through praise, you can find peace for your soul, joy in your spirit, and strength to battle back against his schemes.

Over and over again in the Psalms, we find David praising the Lord. Over and over again in the chronicles of his exploits, we find him winning huge battles and progressing further into his destiny despite the enemy's traps. David understood that when he praised his way into God's presence, he was dwelling in the shelter of the Most High, his rock, his fortress, his deliverer, and his protector from the arrows that fly by day, the terror by night, and the pestilence and destruction. (See Psalm 91.)

Praise is a weapon. Praise is a spiritual warfare tactic straight from heaven that will combat every agenda from hell in your life. Think about it for a minute. Praise brought down the walls at Jericho:

> So the people shouted, and they blew the trumpets. When the people heard the trumpet sound, they shouted a loud battle cry, and the wall fell down. So the people went up

into the city, one man after the other, and they captured it. They destroyed all that was in the city: man and woman, young and old, and oxen, sheep, and donkey with the edge of the sword.

—JOSHUA 6:20–21

Praise also changes our perspective. Instead of becoming devil-minded, you become God-minded. In the heat of the battle we don't ignore the enemy by any means, but sometimes we give glory to him by hyperfocusing on his maneuvers. Praising God recalibrates our focus. When we keep our eyes on God, He'll keep us in perfect peace (Isa. 26:3). We can't help but praise Him when we focus on what He has done in our lives.

Paul and Silas once found themselves in a predicament after the apostle cast a spirit of divination out of a girl who was following them around. When the girl walked free, the people of the city rose in an uproar because it affected their ability to make money. Paul and Silas were beaten and thrown into the depths of the prison, and their feet were fastened in stocks. Now that's a natural manifestation of spiritual warfare! They could have moaned and groaned, but they employed a spiritual warfare tactic that set them free:

> But at midnight Paul and Silas were praying and singing hymns to God, and the prisoners were listening to them. Suddenly there was a great earthquake, so that the foundations of the prison were shaken; and immediately all the doors were opened and everyone's chains were loosed.
>
> —ACTS 16:25–26, NKJV

When the enemy is assaulting you, put on some praise music. Dance, pray, and sing. You will feel joy and strength rising in your heart along with a righteous indignation to fight back!

Spiritual Warfare Tactic 5

WORSHIP *as* WARFARE

Iɴ ᴛʜᴇ ʟᴀsᴛ entry I said when you are in the midst of heavy warfare the last thing you feel like doing is praising the Lord. The second to the last thing you feel like doing is worshipping Him. King Jehoshaphat broke through fear and into worship that worked as warfare. It's a tactic that will work for you too.

Second Chronicles 20 opens with a frightening scene. The Moabites, Ammonites, and Meunites decided to engage in battle with Jehoshaphat. Word came to the king that "a large multitude is coming against you from across the Dead Sea from Edom" (v. 2). The Bible says that Jehoshaphat, understanding the urgency of the matter, "was fearful and set himself to seek the Lᴏʀᴅ, and he called for a fast throughout all Judah. And Judah was assembled to seek the Lᴏʀᴅ; even from all the cities of Judah, they came to obtain aid from the Lᴏʀᴅ" (vv. 3–4).

Facing massive pressure from a fast-approaching army, Jehoshaphat didn't moan, groan, grumble, and complain about the situation he found himself in. He didn't sit and feel sorry for himself and feed his flesh with dainty foods. He didn't jump in bed, pull the covers over his head, and hope the devil would go away. He prayed to the Lord and got a battle tactic called worship.

> Jehoshaphat stood and said, "Listen to me, Judah and those dwelling in Jerusalem. Believe in the Lᴏʀᴅ your God, and you will be supported. Believe His prophets, and you will succeed." And he consulted with the people and then appointed singers for the Lᴏʀᴅ and those praising Him in

holy attire as they went before those equipped for battle saying, "Praise the LORD, for His mercy endures forever."

—2 CHRONICLES 20:20–21

Let's look at how this worship-as-warfare strategy played out in 2 Chronicles 20:22–23:

> When they began singing and praising, the LORD set ambushes against Ammon, Moab, and Mount Seir, who had come against Judah; so they were defeated. Then the Ammonites and Moabites stood up against those dwelling from Mount Seir to destroy and finish them. Then when they made an end of the inhabitants of Seir, each man attacked his companion to destroy each other.

When we engage in worship when all hell is breaking loose against us, it releases confusion into the enemy's camp. Paul understood this all too well. That is why he told the church at Philippi, "Do not be frightened by your adversaries. This is a sign to them of their destruction, but of your salvation, and this from God" (Phil. 1:28).

Look at what happened next with Jehoshaphat and the people of Judah:

> Then Jehoshaphat and his people came to gather their plunder, and they found among them an abundance of riches with the corpses, and precious jewelry, which they took for themselves, more than they could carry. They were gathering the plunder for three days because there was so much to carry. On the fourth day they gathered at the Valley of Berakah, because there they blessed the LORD. For this reason people have called the name of this place the Valley of Berakah until this day.

—2 CHRONICLES 20:25–26

Always remember, when you go to war and win—and you will win when you use God's tactics—you will collect spoils. Worship is a tactic that works when you are facing spiritual warfare.

Spiritual Warfare Tactic 6

PRAY *in* *the* SPIRIT

J UDE, THE HALF-BROTHER of Jesus, gives us a spiritual warfare tactic we would be wise to employ in every battle: "But you, beloved, build yourselves up in your most holy faith. Pray in the Holy Spirit" (Jude 20). The Amplified Classic translation draws out the meaning: "But you, beloved, build yourselves up [founded] on your most holy faith [make progress, rise like an edifice higher and higher], praying in the Holy Spirit."

What does Jude mean? When we are baptized in the Spirit, we get a heavenly prayer language. Paul also shared a marvelous revelation in 1 Corinthians 14:2: "For he who speaks in an unknown tongue does not speak to men, but to God. For no one understands him, although in the spirit, he speaks mysteries." The enemy cannot understand this language—and we can't either unless the Lord reveals to us what we are praying. But know this: it's a direct line to God.

Praying in the Spirit strengthens our inner man. This is strategic since we are not waging war against flesh and blood or by flesh and blood. The spirit man on the inside of us takes the lead in spiritual battles. One way we become stronger in the Lord and the power of His might is to pray in the Spirit. In a so-called apostolic prayer Paul prayed that we would be strengthened in our inner man (Eph. 3:16).

Praying in the Spirit also releases perfect prayers. Romans 8:26 tells us, "Likewise, the Spirit helps us in our weaknesses, for we do not know what to pray for as we ought, but the Spirit Himself intercedes for us with groanings too deep for words."

When we find ourselves overwhelmed with warfare, it becomes hard to pray. The good news is the Holy Spirit is an "Intercessor" (John 14:26, AMPC). When it feels as if your prayers are hitting a glass ceiling and falling back to the ground, pray in the Spirit. You could be praying with Holy Spirit insight to thwart the enemy's strategy against you. You could be praying to dismantle the weapons formed against you.

At times you may feel an unction to pray in the Spirit and find yourself praying in a tongue you've never heard before. I believe that is the Holy Spirit helping you to pray, battling with and for you in the spirit world to oppose enemy attacks underway against you. You may not see the attack coming, but the Holy Spirit sees all things and knows all things. When you feel led to pray in the Spirit, always yield to Him.

Paul continues the revelation in Romans 8:27, "He who searches the hearts knows what the mind of the Spirit is, because He intercedes for the saints according to the will of God."

The Holy Spirit has the mind of God. He always knows the perfect will of the Father and always gets His prayers answered. Let Him help you pray and you will surely tap into the 1 John 5:14–15 promise: "This is the confidence that we have in Him, that if we ask anything according to His will, He hears us. So if we know that He hears whatever we ask, we know that we have whatever we asked of Him."

Spiritual Warfare Tactic 7

PLEAD *the* BLOOD *of* JESUS

W E SING SONGS about the blood of Jesus, but when we truly get a revelation of the power of the blood of Jesus in spiritual warfare, it will revolutionize our faith to fight the good fight. The blood of Jesus washes away our sin. (See Hebrews 10:2–14.)

The blood of Jesus obtained for us eternal redemption and cleanses our conscience from dead works to serve the living God (Eph. 1:7; Heb. 9:12–14). The blood of Jesus justifies us (Rom. 5:9), reconciles us (Col. 1:19–20), and sanctifies us (Heb. 13:12). The shed blood of Christ secured for us an eternal covenant with Father God (Heb. 13:20). Jesus purchased the church with His own blood (Acts 20:28). We have confidence to enter the holy place by the blood of Jesus (Heb. 10:19–22).

In relation to taking Communion, Jesus said, "For this is My blood of the new covenant, which is shed for many for the remission of sins" (Matt. 26:28). When we plead the blood of Jesus, we are pleading our rights under the new covenant. Our new covenant rights include assurance that nothing separates us from His love (Rom. 8:39), that we are righteous in Christ (2 Cor. 5:21), that the Holy Spirit will help us (John 14:26), that God is with us and we can approach Him with confidence (Eph. 3:12), that God is on our side (Rom. 8:31), and that He has empowered us to overcome the enemy (1 John 5:4).

Some argue pleading the blood of Jesus is not scriptural because they cannot find chapter and verse in the Bible, but there are nearly forty scriptures speaking about the blood of Jesus. The enemy cringes at the blood of Jesus because the shed blood of Christ paved the way for our designated authority over the enemy's kingdom of darkness. When we plead the blood of Jesus, we are appealing to the mercy of God and declaring our position in Christ to the enemy of our souls. That's why a revelation of the power of the blood is so vital to walking in victory.

In legal terms pleading the blood is like a lawyer pleading his case before a judge. In our own right we can't stand against the devil. When the accuser of the brethren attacks us, the blood of Jesus is our defense and authorizes us to push back the darkness trying to invade our lives. Thanks to the precious blood of Jesus, the enemy has no legal right to wreak havoc in our lives any longer.

Practically speaking, I plead the blood of Jesus over myself, my family, my friends, my ministry, my finances, and everything I'm involved with each and every day. I don't do this as a rote exercise. I plead the blood of Christ because I understand its power.

BREAK
WORD CURSES

Y OU HAVE BEEN redeemed from the curse of the law, but that doesn't mean you are immune to word curses. The Bible says the power of death and life are in the tongue (Prov. 18:21). A word curse is essentially the power of death emanating toward you from someone's tongue. Whether intentional or not, word curses work to inflict harm on your body, bring damage to your soul, or otherwise work against God's plan for your life.

The devil can use well-intentioned people who love you to release word curses over you. People who are jealous of you—or otherwise don't like you—can release word curses over you. You can even release word curses over yourself. Word curses can take the form of insults, false accusations, judgments, or confessions of death over your life, such as "I always get sick this time of year" or "He will never hold down a job."

Proverbs 12:18 reveals there are those who "speak like the piercings of a sword." Proverbs 15:4 tells us, "A wholesome tongue is a tree of life, but perverseness in it crushes the spirit." Proverbs 11:9 reveals, "A hypocrite with his mouth destroys his neighbor, but through knowledge the just will be delivered." And Proverbs 25:18 says, "A man who bears false witness against his neighbor is like a club, a sword, and a sharp arrow."

James 3:8 tells us the tongue is an unruly evil that is full of deadly poison. Strong words! Paul warned us to bless and curse not (Rom. 12:14). When we curse anything, we speak ill of it. Think about it for a minute. When Jesus cursed the fig tree, it withered up. (See Mark 11:12–14, 20–25.) Studies show that when we talk to plants, they react.[1] If you say nice things to plants, they thrive. If you curse the plants, they suffer.

Word curses from authority figures in our lives seem to carry more weight because we put more stock in them—we accept them. As youth, when our parents continually tell us we are stupid and will never amount to anything, those curses linger over us. They must be broken. Ultimately, though, we believe what we say about ourselves more than what anyone else says about us. The most powerful word curses, then, are self-curses.

Breaking word curses means repenting if you cursed yourself and renouncing curses if they came through the mouth of another. At times you may sense word curses in the spirit realm and never really know from whom they originated. It's not as important that you discern who is cursing you as it is to discern the working of the curse.

Practically speaking, I break every word curse, hex, vex, spell, incantation, potion, and expression of witchcraft coming against me, my daughter, my family, my business, my ministry, my finances, and everything that relates to me, in Jesus's name. Jesus redeemed you from the curse of the law, being made a curse for you (Gal. 3:13). You have authority to break word curses and to release the opposite of the curse—blessings over your life for His glory.

CAST DOWN IMAGINATIONS

PAUL TAUGHT US the concept of casting down imaginations, but many believers don't understand how to engage in this type of mind warfare. Second Corinthians 10:5 lays out the concept: "Casting down imaginations, and every high thing that exalteth itself against the knowledge of God, and bringing into captivity every thought to the obedience of Christ" (KJV).

The Amplified Classic translation breaks it down in finer detail: "[Inasmuch as we] refute arguments and theories and reasonings and every proud and lofty thing that sets itself up against the [true] knowledge of God; and we lead every thought and purpose away captive into the obedience of Christ (the Messiah, the Anointed One)."

As you seek to cast down fearful imaginations—or any imaginations that exalt themselves against the knowledge of God—it is helpful to understand that the phrase *casting down* in that verse comes from the Greek word *kathairéō*, which has a violent connotation. *Kathairéō* means "take down for oneself; forcibly yank down; destroy (demolish), leaving nothing 'standing,' or even in good working order; cast down."[1] It also means to cast down "with the use of force."[2]

The Bible says you are to cast down every imagination, not just some imaginations. The battle is in your mind, but the war is for your heart. When thoughts that oppose God's Word plague you, decide to evict them with the full force of your will. That begins by paying attention to your thought life. You have to think about what you are thinking about.

Here's a practical example: When you have a thought such as, "I'll never succeed at anything," you know that is not the Lord speaking to you. The Holy Spirit does not speak to you in terms of failure because there is no failure in Christ. You must first recognize the thought as a vain imagination that is exalting itself above God's Word. Next, you have to take that thought captive. Out of your holy mouth, you would say, "I reject the thought that I will never succeed. I bind that vain imagination in the name of Jesus."

Don't stop there. Speak the opposite out of your mouth according to the Word of God. In this case you would say, "No one who hopes in the Lord will ever be put to shame (Ps. 25:3). I put my trust in the Lord who always leads me into triumph in Christ Jesus (2 Cor. 2:14). I thank You, Lord, that You give me confidence to pursue the dreams You have put in my heart, in Jesus's name."

The idea is you never cast down without lifting up the Word of God. You don't bind without loosing. You don't just eradicate a wrong thought; you replace it with the right thought. You may have to do this over and over again with fearful thoughts because we never defeat fear once and for all. Fear is always roaming about like a roaring lion looking to devour your wild dreams. But you can submit yourself to God, resist fear, and force it to flee (James 4:7).

PUT ON YOUR
SHOES *of* PEACE

P AUL OUTLINED THE whole armor of God in Ephesians 6. Each
element is strategic in your war against the wicked one. The shoes
of peace are often overlooked in the context of spiritual warfare,
but make no mistake, walking in peace is a battle tactic that drives
the devil mad.

In Ephesians 6:15 Paul tells us to have our "feet fitted with the
readiness of the gospel of peace." Other translations speak of the
"shoes" of peace (e.g., ESV) or having our feet "shod" (e.g., KJV). The
idea is to walk in the peace of God, about which the Bible has
plenty to say.

Jesus makes it clear in Scripture He has not left us without
help. The Father sent the Holy Spirit to be our helper after Jesus
ascended to heaven. Jesus said, "I have told you these things so
that in Me you may have peace. In the world you will have distress.
But be of good cheer. I have overcome the world" (John 16:33). Paul
promises us if we pray and thank God, the result will be supernatural peace that passes all understanding—and that peace will
guard our hearts and minds in Christ Jesus (Phil. 4:6–7).

We know that our hope and faith in God will fill us with joy
and peace (Rom. 15:13). Paul explains that "To be carnally minded
is death, but to be spiritually minded is life and peace" (Rom. 8:6)
and encourages us to "let the peace of God, to which also you are
called in one body, rule in your hearts" (Col. 3:15). The kingdom of
God, after all, is righteousness, peace, and joy in the Holy Ghost
(Rom. 14:17).

In the Old Testament we find this promise: "You will keep him in perfect peace, whose mind is stayed on You, because he trusts in You" (Isa. 26:3). God also promises, "For the mountains may be removed, and the hills may shake, but My kindness shall not depart from you, nor shall My covenant of peace be removed, says the LORD who has mercy on you" (Isa. 54:10).

Ecclesiastes 3:8 tells us there is a time for war and a time for peace. But I can testify that you can have peace in the middle of the war when you understand who you are in Christ.

See, the devil is not really after your money, because he can't use your money. The devil is not really after your car or your job or your house. No, not really. He's after your peace, your joy, your hope, and your faith. He wants to spoil the fruit of the Spirit— love, joy, peace, patience, gentleness, goodness, faith, meekness, and self-control—in your life by tempting you to walk in the flesh.

Decide each day to put on your shoes of peace. Make a decision that nothing is going to steal the peace Jesus gave you. Choose to stay peaceful when the enemy is hitting you with his best shot. Seek peace with everyone around you, even when they are striving against you. Hold your peace!

PUT ON YOUR BREASTPLATE
of RIGHTEOUSNESS

ONE OF THE enemy's key spiritual warfare strategies is to attack your identity in Christ. After all, if the devil can get you to waver on who you are in Him—and your right standing in Him—he can cause you to lay down the rest of your weapons so he can come in for the kill.

Paul admonishes us to put on the breastplate of righteousness (Eph. 6:14). The New Living Translation puts it this way: "the body armor of God's righteousness." And the Amplified Classic translation describes it as "breastplate of integrity and of moral rectitude and right standing with God."

Let's think about what this really means. A breastplate is the part of the armor that protects a large portion of your body—from the neck to the navel. Most fatal wounds are hits to this area of the body. Righteousness protects you from the devil's cheap shots against your heart, so it's vital to put on this heavy metal defensive armor.

Your own righteousness is like "filthy rags" (Isa. 64:6). Self-righteousness won't take you anywhere in spiritual warfare. We stand on 2 Corinthians 5:21: "God made Him who knew no sin to be sin for us, that we might become the righteousness of God in Him."

What does it mean to become the righteousness of God in Christ? The Greek word *righteousness* in 2 Corinthians 5:21 is *dikaiosynē*. It means "in a broad sense: state of him who is as he ought to be, righteousness, the condition acceptable to God; the doctrine concerning the way in which man may attain a state approved of God; integrity, virtue, purity of life, rightness, correctness of thinking, feeling, and acting; in a narrower sense, justice or the virtue which gives each his due."[1]

The enemy works to bring a sin consciousness to your soul. You must strive to maintain a righteousness consciousness and ward off guilt, condemnation, and shame that try to creep into your mind and emotions when you sin. If this happens, remember Romans 8:1, "There is therefore now no condemnation for those who are in Christ Jesus, who walk not according to the flesh, but according to the Spirit."

You won't fight when you feel condemned. You won't fight when you feel guilty. You won't fight when you feel ashamed of yourself. You must choose to put on the breastplate of righteousness and keep it on. If you sin, don't throw off your armor. Instead, run to the Lord and ask Him to secure it. Repent and ask Him for the grace to resist temptations.

Spiritual Warfare Tactic 12

PUT ON YOUR
HELMET *of* SALVATION

No football player in his right mind would step on the field without his helmet. Likewise, no soldier in the army of God should enter the mission field—or the battlefield—without the helmet of salvation. Indeed, the Bible speaks of this helmet three times. Beyond Paul's exhortation in Ephesians 6:17 to "take the helmet of salvation," we see Isaiah speak of the helmet of salvation (Isa. 59:17) and Paul again speak about the hope of salvation as a helmet (1 Thess. 5:8).

Let's dig deeper into this helmet analogy and how to practically put it on—and keep it on—in the midst of the battle. *Merriam-Webster* defines *helmet* as "a covering or enclosing headpiece of ancient or medieval armor; any of various protective head coverings usually made of a hard material to resist impact."[1]

Think about that for a minute. The helmet is to cover, or protect, your head to resist impact. A shot to the arms and legs isn't usually fatal, but a shot to the head can kill you instantly. The enemy's thoughts aim to impact your soul—your mind, will, and emotions. The enemy's fiery darts work to reason your mind out of God's protection, bend your will away from His plans, and send you on the emotional roller coaster called instability. Your mind commands your body, so if your mind falters in the attack, the enemy can paralyze you.

The Greek word for helmet in Ephesians 6:17 is *perikephalaia*, which means "helmet," but it is also a metaphor for "the protection of the soul which consists in (the hope of) salvation."[2] *Salvation* in this verse, in turn, is the Greek word *sōtērios*. One of the definitions is "saving, bringing salvation."[3] Through faith in Jesus Christ, you are saved, you are being saved, and you will be saved.

Put another way, God delivered you from the kingdom of darkness into the kingdom of light (Col. 1:13). But He didn't leave you in this world to work out your salvation with fear and trembling about the devil's plans for your life. He didn't leave you here to be tossed to and fro by the wicked one's attacks on your mind until one day He takes you up to heaven. No, He has given you the helmet of salvation to securely fasten around your soul now.

If you put it on, the helmet of salvation will guard your mind from the wicked one's assaults, which include guilt and condemnation when you miss the mark. If you put it on, the helmet of salvation will give you confidence of God's saving grace in the midst of the battle. But you have to put it on—and keep it on.

So, how do you put on the helmet of salvation? Practically speaking, you renew your mind to the power of the Cross. Meditate on what salvation really means. The Greek word for salvation can mean "welfare, prosperity, deliverance, preservation, salvation, or safety."[4] That covers just about every area the enemy works to kill, steal, and destroy. When you are settled that God is your Savior, the devil's mind traffic hits a red light.

WIELD *the* SWORD
of the SPIRIT

In Ephesians 6:17 Paul exhorts us to take up the "sword of the Spirit, which is the word of God." He didn't mean to carry it around as a fashion statement like a cross on a necklace or a T-shirt with a Bible verse. There's certainly nothing wrong with these displays of faith, but they don't combat the enemy's assignments against you. No, Paul meant to be prepared to wield the sword of the Spirit in the heat of the good fight of faith.

The Aramaic New Testament in Plain English tells us to "grasp the sword of the Spirit" while GOD'S WORD Translation speaks of "God's word as the sword that the Spirit supplies." I also like the Amplified Bible, Classic Edition's translation because it reveals how God Himself helps us fight our battles. It speaks of "the sword that the Spirit wields, which is the Word of God."

Before Jesus set out to fulfill His mission, He was baptized in the Holy Spirit. Suddenly the Spirit drove Him into the wilderness, "where He was tempted (tried, tested exceedingly) by the devil" (Luke 4:2, AMPC). When the devil started tempting Jesus, we see the perfect example of how the Holy Spirit cooperates with us to wield His sword, which is the Word of God. Three times Jesus picked up His sword in Luke 4:3–12:

> The devil said to Him, "If You are the Son of God, command this stone to become bread."
>
> Jesus answered him, "It is written, 'Man shall not live by bread alone, but by every word of God.'"
>
> The devil, taking Him up onto a high mountain, showed Him all the kingdoms of the world in a moment of time.

And the devil said to Him, "I will give You all this power and their glory, for it has been delivered to me. And I give it to whomever I will. If You, then, will worship me, all will be Yours."

And Jesus answered and said to him, "Get behind Me, Satan! For it is written, 'You shall worship the Lord your God, and Him only shall you serve.'"

He brought Him to Jerusalem, set Him on the pinnacle of the temple, and said to Him, "If You are the Son of God, throw Yourself down from here. For it is written: 'He shall give His angels charge concerning you, to preserve you,' and 'In their hands they shall hold you up, lest you strike your foot against a stone.'"

Jesus answered him, "It is said, 'You shall not tempt the Lord your God.'"

When you find yourself under enemy attack, pick up the sword of the Spirit immediately. If you cannot do anything more than hold your Bible and read it out loud, saying, "It is written," do it—and do not stop until you get hold of your mind. Merely speaking God's Word out of your mouth will help you gird up the loins of your mind and enable the Holy Spirit to break in and speak to your heart with truth that will set you free from enemy attack.

In different seasons, especially seasons of heavy combat, I mentally walk through the Ephesians 6 armor of God, putting on each piece one by one. This is one way to wield the sword of the Spirit as an offensive measure, helping remind yourself that you have weapons of warfare and putting the enemy on notice that you are dressed for battle.

TIGHTEN YOUR
BELT *of* TRUTH

T RUTH IS A weapon, but it is also a defense against the lies of the enemy. Satan is the father of lies, and he works in the realm of deception. Therefore, it's important that you, as Paul wrote, have "your waist girded with truth" (Eph. 6:14).

Other translations say: "with the belt of truth buckled around your waist" (NIV); "putting on the belt of truth" (NLT); "having fastened on the belt of truth" (ESV); "with truth like a belt around your waist" (HCSB); and "having the utility belt of truth buckled around your waist" (WEB).

Consider the purpose of a belt. Belts carry tools. The weapons of your warfare must be aligned with truth. In other words, what you have learned about warring in the Spirit must be accurate. You need to pursue accuracy in the Word and in the spirit.

Belts can be worn as a symbol of victory, such as when a boxer wins the world championship. Truth says Jesus is our victory, and we are merely executing His win. When waging warfare against the enemy, truth is paramount to walking in victory because when you know the truth and walk in the truth, that truth will set you free (John 8:32). The Word is truth (John 17:17). The Holy Spirit will lead you into all truth because He is the Spirit of truth (John 16:13). You can't take off the belt of truth even for a minute. In fact, you need to buckle it a notch tighter in times of great onslaught. Buckle it so tight that it squeezes out any lies from the enemy of your soul that you have accepted as truth.

Understand and know this: the enemy will work hard to get you to loosen your belt of truth, to compromise the truth so he has an open door of attack. The enemy ultimately wants you to abandon the truth of who you are in Christ, what belongs to you as a believer, and the victory Christ won at Calvary. You must hold tightly to the truth in the face of warfare.

Many recall the blockbuster movie *A Few Good Men* starring Jack Nicholson and Tom Cruise. Colonel Nathan R. Jessup (Nicholson) was on the stand as Lieutenant Daniel Kaffee (Cruise) questioned him about whether he ordered a code red, a violent, extrajudicial punishment. Kaffee insisted he was entitled to the truth. Jessup declared, "You can't handle the truth."[1]

The enemy can't handle the truth. Hold fast to the truth when lies are hitting your mind. Tighten the belt of truth when it seems the enemy's plans are overtaking God's promises in your life. Jesus is the truth, the way, and the life, and standing on His truth when you've done all you can do will eventually cause the devil to flee.

Spiritual Warfare Tactic 15

LIFT UP YOUR
SHIELD *of* FAITH

T HE WRITER OF Hebrews assures us, "Now faith is the substance of things hoped for, the evidence of things not seen" (Heb. 11:1). And Paul tells us to take "the shield of faith, with which you will be able to extinguish all the fiery arrows of the evil one" (Eph. 6:16).

We can't see God. We can't see the weapons of our warfare, which "are not carnal, but mighty through God for the pulling down of strongholds" (2 Cor. 10:4). We can't see the enemies of our souls, and we can't see our shields of faith. Nevertheless, we know all these things exist. We know that the spiritual realm is more real than the natural realm. We walk by faith and not by sight (2 Cor. 5:7).

Faith produces. We can put a demand on our faith to create a shield—a force field, if you will—against the wicked one's attacks. Put another way, faith is a substance that creates a shield against enemy attack. Our faith is not based in our spiritual warfare skills or the prayers of our pastor. Our faith is not based in our ability to quote Scripture. Our faith is based in the hope of God's protection and deliverance.

This fervent faith—faith based purely on God and His Word—is a shield that is able to extinguish all the fiery darts of the evil one. After listing other pieces of the armor of God, Paul says to lift up the shield of faith "above all" (Eph. 6:16). Faith is what activates or energizes the rest of our armor. If we don't believe our armor is effective, it won't be. If we don't put on our armor by faith, we'll run into war ill-prepared to absorb the enemy's hits.

I've heard people say their arms sometimes grow tired of holding up the shield of faith, that it gets so heavy they are tempted to put it down. I know the feeling. I think we've all been there. Even Moses's arms grew weary in the midst of the battle. As long as Moses's arms were lifted, the Israelites advanced in battle. When Moses's arms fell, the Israelites started losing ground, so Aaron and Hur helped lift up his arms. (See Exodus 17:8–16.)

Moses's experience serves as a prophetic picture of what happens when we let our shield of faith sink in the face of weariness. The good news is the Holy Spirit can strengthen our arms and indeed helps us to hold our shield of faith when we refuse to give up. Just like Moses had natural help, we have a supernatural helper named Holy Spirit who empowers us to stand and withstand in the evil day.

When we put our faith in God and His Word, we can rest assured that God's Word will work for us. So how do we keep our shield lifted up in the midst of a long, arduous battle? By feeding our spirit with the Word of God. Romans 10:17 says, "So then faith comes by hearing, and hearing by the word of God." When you are in the midst of a battle, find scriptures that relate to your specific situation and let them produce the faith that builds your strength to hold up your shield.

RUN *to* YOUR OWN COMPANY

THE BIBLE SPEAKS of those who are of "like precious faith" (2 Pet. 1:1, NKJV). Technically all those who name Jesus as Lord and Savior are of like precious faith in the sense that we are the body of Christ. Still, there are many debates over issues that do not relate directly to salvation, including warfare doctrines.

When you are under siege, it's important to run to your own company. We see this illustrated in Acts 4 after Peter and John healed the man at the Beautiful Gate. The dynamic duo was arrested for preaching Jesus with signs following. The priests, rulers of the temple, and Sadducees gathered together and ultimately commanded them not to speak or teach in the name of Jesus. When Peter refused to bow to their orders, the rulers issued further threats. But "on being released, [Peter and John] went to their own people and reported what the chief priests and elders had said to them. When they heard this, they lifted their voices in unity to God and prayed" (Acts 4:23–24). Other translations say they "went to their own company" (KJV), "went to their own companions" (NKJV), or "returned to their own [people]" (AMP).

When arrested and threatened—when they were under enemy attack for doing the will of the Lord—they didn't run and hide in a cave. They returned to their own company, to people they could trust and who would pray for them. They sought the support of those who believed the same as they did and who would lift up their arms in the battle.

It's important to note the enemy doesn't just use unseen forces or unbelievers to accuse, threaten, and attack you for doing God's will. Indeed, sometimes you're under siege by those who believe in the same God but reject your beliefs on miracles, signs, wonders, healings, the Holy Spirit, spiritual gifts, and spiritual warfare. That's why you don't just run to a phone and call a random prayer line for prayer support. You run to your own company.

What type of prayer did these unified believers in Acts 4 pray? Did they bind and loose? Did they push back darkness? Did they come against the devil's schemes? They could have, but they prayed a corporate prayer knowing that the attacks that came against Peter and John were likely to manifest against them all since they held fast to the same beliefs—to the like precious faith. Hear their prayer:

> "Now, Lord, look on their threats and grant that Your servants may speak Your word with great boldness, by stretching out Your hand to heal and that signs and wonders may be performed in the name of Your holy Son Jesus." When they had prayed, the place where they were assembled together was shaken. And they were all filled with the Holy Spirit and spoke the word of God with boldness.
>
> —ACTS 4:29–31

When you are under attack, it's not time to break rank. It's time to run back to your own company, to your church, to your pastors, to your friends who will stand with you. There's something about that corporate anointing that sets the stage for unity and allows the Holy Spirit to manifest with deliverance, refreshing, wisdom, and power.

REPENT: STRIP *the* ENEMY'S RIGHTS

Iᶠ ʏᴏᴜ ᴀʀᴇ practicing sin, you won't successfully maintain victory over the enemy. We see this principle under Joshua's leadership when Achan violated the word of the Lord, took some of the spoils of war, and hid them underground in his tent. His sin opened a door to great casualties in Israel's next battle. (See Joshua 7.) From this account we learn the principle of repenting before going into battle. Never enter into warfare without first entering into repentance for personal sin.

> Who may ascend the mountain of the Lᴏʀᴅ? Who may stand in his holy place? The one who has clean hands and a pure heart, who does not trust in an idol or swear by a false god. They will receive blessing from the Lᴏʀᴅ and vindication from God their Savior.
> —Psᴀʟᴍ 24:3–5, ɴɪᴠ

> He who covers his sins will not prosper, but whoever confesses and forsakes them will have mercy.
> —Pʀᴏᴠᴇʀʙs 28:13

John the Baptist preached, "Repent, for the kingdom of heaven is at hand" (Matt. 3:2). The word *repent* is from the Greek word *metanoeō*, which means "to change one's mind, i.e. to repent; to change one's mind for better, heartily to amend with abhorrence of one's past sins."[1]

True repentance means a change of heart about the sin you've committed—seeing it the way God sees it, renouncing it, and turning away from it. Paul the apostle breaks it down scripturally and contrasts worldly sorry with godly sorrow in a powerful way in 2 Corinthians 7:8–12 (NKJV):

> For even if I made you sorry with my letter, I do not regret it; though I did regret it. For I perceive that the same epistle made you sorry, though only for a while. Now I rejoice, not that you were made sorry, but that your sorrow led to repentance. For you were made sorry in a godly manner, that you might suffer loss from us in nothing. For godly sorrow produces repentance leading to salvation, not to be regretted; but the sorrow of the world produces death. For observe this very thing, that you sorrowed in a godly manner: What diligence it produced in you, what clearing of yourselves, what indignation, what fear, what vehement desire, what zeal, what vindication! In all things you proved yourselves to be clear in this matter. Therefore, although I wrote to you, I did not do it for the sake of him who had done the wrong, nor for the sake of him who suffered wrong, but that our care for you in the sight of God might appear to you.

Don't let this call to repentance offend you. Heed the warning and the good news of John, the apostle of love, in 1 John 1:8–10: "If we say that we have no sin, we deceive ourselves, and the truth is not in us. If we confess our sins, He is faithful and just to forgive us our sins and cleanse us from all unrighteousness. If we say that we have not sinned, we make Him a liar and His word is not in us."

We all fall short of the glory of God every day. Repentance itself can cause the warfare to stop because we are resisting the devil and submitting ourselves to God. When we do this, according to James 4:7, the devil has to flee.

ENCOURAGE YOURSELF *in the* LORD

I ALWAYS APPRECIATE AN encouraging word, but sometimes there's no one around to encourage me. In fact, sometimes those who should be encouraging me are discouraging me! The enemy can use the people closest to us to bring the greatest warfare at times. I've learned to take a page out of David's playbook and encourage myself in the Lord.

We find David and his mighty men in great distress in 1 Samuel 30. When he and his crew went back to their camp at Ziklag, they discovered the Amalekites raided them and burned the city down. Their enemies also kidnapped the women and children. Even David's wives were taken captive. David and all his men cried until they couldn't cry anymore.

Then it got worse: "David was greatly distressed, for the people talked of stoning him, because all the people were bitter in spirit, each over his sons and daughters. But David encouraged himself in the Lord his God" (1 Sam. 30:6).

Even for the strongest of heart, this was a discouraging situation. Part of the enemy's assignment to kill, steal, and destroy is discouragement. Thankfully David didn't wallow in self-pity. He rose like a leader and got himself together. I imagine he stole away for a few minutes to gather himself and pray. I can just see David down on his knees, crying out to God. I can almost hear his prayer:

> I will bless the Lord at all times; His praise will continually be in my mouth. My soul will make its boast in the Lord; the humble will hear of it and be glad. Oh, magnify the Lord with me, and let us exalt His name together.

I sought the LORD, and He answered me, and delivered me from all my fears. They looked to Him and became radiant, and their faces are not ashamed. This poor man cried, and the LORD heard, and saved him out of all his troubles. The angel of the LORD camps around those who fear Him, and delivers them.

Oh, taste and see that the LORD is good; blessed is the man who takes refuge in Him. Oh, fear the LORD, you His saints; for the ones who fear Him will not be in need. The young lions are in want and suffer hunger, but the ones who seek the LORD will not lack any good thing.

—PSALM 34:1–10

I believe David reminded himself of God's faithfulness, His delivering power, His sustaining grace, His direction in battle. When you can't find anyone else to encourage you, encourage yourself in the Lord. In other words, remind yourself of who the Lord is to you. Reading the psalms of David is a strategic prayer strategy in times of discouragement in warfare.

Many times when you're under heavy attack and discouraged, you feel as if no one else can possibly understand you. Jesus understands you—and I believe David does too. If anyone understands what it is like to be hunted down, chased around, betrayed, and otherwise attacked, it's David. David cried out to the Lord with great transparency about his emotions but always encouraged himself in the Lord's faithfulness.

REMIND *the* DEVIL *of* PAST VICTORIES

W E DON'T WANT to live in the past, but we can use the past to our advantage in spiritual warfare. We can remind the devil—and ourselves—of past victories in battle. We see David walking in this principle in 1 Samuel 17:33–37 when King Saul looked through natural eyes at a ruddy teenager who seemed ill-prepared to defeat a giant named Goliath who left all the Israelite army trembling in their boots:

> Saul said to David, "You are not able to go against this Philistine to fight with him. For you are but a youth, and he has been a man of war from his youth."
>
> David said to Saul, "Your servant was a shepherd for my father's flock, and the lion came and the bear, and took a lamb out of the flock. And I went out after him, and struck him, and delivered it out of his mouth. And when he arose against me, I took hold of his beard, struck him, and killed him. Your servant slew both the lion and the bear. And this uncircumcised Philistine will be as one of them, because he has reviled the armies of the living God." David said, "The LORD who delivered me out of the paw of the lion and out of the paw of the bear, He will deliver me out of the hand of this Philistine."

Hallelujah! David reminded himself of—and essentially declared in the spirit realm—his past victories. Reminding the devil of your past wins against him builds your faith to overcome in your current battle. If God delivered you once, He'll deliver you again!

When the Israelites finally entered the Promised Land, God instructed them to build a monument to remind them of His saving grace. Just as the Lord parted the Red Sea under Moses's leadership so the children of Israel could escape Pharaoh and his army, the Lord parted the waters at the River Jordan so they could move into the Promised Land on dry ground.

> When your children ask, "What do these stones mean to you?" you will answer them that the waters of the Jordan were cut off before the ark of the covenant of the LORD. When it crossed the Jordan, the waters of the Jordan were cut off. These stones will be a memorial for the children of Israel continually.
>
> —JOSHUA 4:6–7

If you've overcome some big mountains in your life, this strategy of reminding the devil of past victories works especially well. I've been through so many things—both as a lost soul and as an on-fire believer—that it takes a lot to move me at this point. When you have a history in God, it's harder for the enemy to rattle you as he battles you. A little cold-and-flu devil won't stop you from going to church anymore. A flat tire won't send you into a tizzy. A financial storm won't keep you from giving.

Even if you don't have much history with God, the Bible is full of accounts of people in desperate situations who put their trust in the Lord and saw victory in battle. Time and time again, the Lord gives victory to His people when they trust in Him.

WAGE WAR WITH *the* PROPHETIC WORDS OVER YOUR LIFE

Paul gave his spiritual son Timothy a key strategy: "This command I commit to you, my son Timothy, according to the prophecies that were previously given to you, that by them you might fight a good fight" (1 Tim. 1:18). The Amplified translation of that verse exhorts us to be "inspired and aided" by the prophetic words so that, according to the Amplified Classic, "you may wage the good warfare." The New Living Translation tells us that the prophetic words "help you fight well in the Lord's battles." And The Message paraphrase tells us the prophecies should make you "fearless in your struggle, keeping a firm grip on your faith and on yourself. After all, this is a fight we're in."

Most personal prophecy is conditional. You have to cooperate with God to see His will come to pass. Praying out the prophecies you've received is a keen strategy from the Bible, but you should not start praying out prophecies that have not first been judged. I write about this topic extensively in my book *Did the Spirit of God Say That?* In general, though, prophetic words can be traced back to any one of three sources: the human spirit (Jer. 23:16), an evil spirit (Jer. 23:13), or the Holy Spirit (2 Pet. 1:21).

You're fighting a good fight of faith more than you're fighting any enemy. The enemy is real, but the fight is often the fight to believe God's Word is true in the face of contrary circumstances. Scripture is the final authority and your sword, but tested prophetic words are like arrows in your quiver that you can shoot into the spirit realm to hit the target of God's revealed will. It's time to go back and review some of your prophetic words and rise up against the enemies standing in the way of your destiny.

How do you war with a prophetic word? How do you step into that 1 Timothy 1:18 reality? Practically speaking, you pray through it line by line. Suppose you get a prophetic word that says this: "I am preparing you to be a vessel of change in your city. I am calling you to make an impact in your region. I am equipping you to press in to new levels of My glory so that you can carry My presence into dark territories."

After you meditate on it and confess it out of your mouth, you would pray it out in a manner such as this:

> *I thank You, Lord, that You are preparing me to be a vessel of change in my city. I thank You for the opportunity to serve You in this way, and I yield to Your preparation. Lord, show me what You need me to do to cooperate with You and to prepare myself for this mission, and give me the grace to do it. Thank You for this calling to make an impact on my region. Lord, please give me strategies and tactics and send laborers to work alongside me. Thank You that You are equipping me to press in to new levels of Your glory. Show me Your glory. Show me how to carry Your presence into dark territories for Your glory. Show me what steps to take. Lead me and guide me by Your Spirit, in the name of Jesus.*

Spiritual Warfare Tactic 21

ENGAGE *in the* PRAYER *of* AGREEMENT

Iᴛ's ʙᴇᴇɴ sᴀɪᴅ there's strength in numbers, and the Bible proves it. There is power in agreement. Engage in the prayer of agreement, whether it's with one other person or with a group of people, and you'll increase your spiritual firepower exponentially.

Jesus assures us, "Again I say to you, that if two of you agree on earth about anything they ask, it will be done for them by My Father who is in heaven. For where two or three are assembled in My name, there I am in their midst" (Matt. 18:19–20).

This reminds me of Psalm 68:1: "Let God arise, let His enemies be scattered; let those who hate Him flee before Him." When we make room for God, when we pray in unity, He will rise up in our midst and fight with us.

Now, the key to Matthew 18:19 is true agreement. You have to pray with a person—or with people—who really agrees. If your prayer partner's heart is not aligned with yours in the matter, you aren't truly tapping into the promise. If your prayer partner is judging you in her heart, the prayer will hit the ceiling and fall back to the ground. If the person doesn't have faith to see the prayer answer, that's not doing you much good either. When you engage in the prayer of agreement, find someone who really, truly agrees.

In corporate warfare we lean on a scripture that embraces a similar principle. Joshua 23:10 tells us, "One man from among you can make one thousand flee, for it is the Lᴏʀᴅ your God who wages war for you, as He told you." And Deuteronomy 32:30 offers some divine math I appreciate: "How should one chase one thousand,

and two put ten thousand to flight, unless their rock had sold them, and the LORD had given them up?"

Ultimately the battle is the Lord's, and He is fighting for us. Nevertheless there's the principle of agreement and a corporate anointing where we can do more damage to the enemy's kingdom together than we can alone.

Again, there is strength in numbers. There is synergy that cannot be denied. Two people could carry a couch that one person could never carry alone. Two people can carry far more weight together than either could individually. It's a multiplication effect based on unity. Where the Lord finds unity, there's a yoke-breaking anointing and a blessing from heaven. (See Psalm 133.)

Keep in mind there are some battles the Lord will let you fight alone because you need to learn a certain principle to carry you to the next level. You need to learn how to take authority over things in your own right. But even then you are not alone. The Lord is on your side, and if God is for you, who can be against you (Rom. 8:31)? And what does it matter who is against you when the Lord is with you?

REFUSE *to* MEDITATE ON *the* DEVIL'S FALSE PROPHECIES

Tʜᴇ ᴅᴇᴠɪʟ ɪs a false prophet. In other words, he prophesies lies to your heart. The devil prophesies about failure in your present and doom and gloom in your future. He prophesies to you about your health, your family, your finances, and your destiny. Satan has been a liar from the beginning. He's the father of lies and the propagator of false prophecies against your life.

When Nehemiah was rebuilding the wall around Jerusalem, his enemies sent someone to prophesy against him: "Then I perceived and saw that God had not sent him, but that he pronounced the prophecy against me, because Tobiah and Sanballat had hired him. He was hired for this reason: that I might become fearful, act accordingly, and sin. Then they would have an evil report by which they could reproach me" (Neh. 6:12–13).

From this incident we learn the enemy will use people to prophesy falsely over you with intimidation tactics that work to send you running away from the Lord's will. But we have another example in David's battle against Goliath. The giant himself prophesied against David. We read the account in 1 Samuel 17:42–44:

> When the Philistine looked and saw David, he despised him. For he was a youth and ruddy with a handsome appearance. The Philistine said to David, "Am I a dog, that you come to me with sticks?" Then the Philistine cursed David by his gods. The Philistine said to David, "Come to me, and I will give your flesh to the birds of the heavens and to the beasts of the field."

The devil will also prophesy directly to your mind in a still, small voice of condemnation. The enemy will confirm his false prophecies by sending others across your path to discourage your heart or by beating the same drum in your soul. When you meditate on these false prophecies, you start conforming to the image they hold in your mind. The Bible says, "As [a man] thinks in his heart, so is he" (Prov. 23:7).

Instead of receiving and meditating on the devil's false prophecies, do like David did and prophesy back to the devil. I love this passage from 1 Samuel 17:45–47:

> Then David said to the Philistine, "You come to me with a sword, a spear, and a shield, but I come to you in the name of the LORD of Hosts, the God of the armies of Israel, whom you have reviled. This day will the LORD deliver you into my hand. And I will strike you down and cut off your head. Then I will give the corpses of the Philistine camp this day to the birds of the air and to the beasts of the earth so that all the earth may know that there is a God in Israel. And then all this assembly will know that it is not by sword and spear that the LORD saves. For the battle belongs to the LORD, and He will give you into our hands."

When the devil prophesies that you can't pay your mortgage, prophesy back: "My God shall supply all my needs according to His riches in glory in Christ Jesus" (Phil. 4:19). When he prophesies you'll never be healed, prophesy back: "By His stripes I am healed" (Isa. 53:5). When he prophesies your prodigal child will never return, prophesy back: "I raised my child in the way he should go, and when he is old, he will not depart from it" (Prov. 22:6). Don't meditate on the devil's prophecies. Prophesy back to him!

STAY FILLED
WITH *the* SPIRIT

IT'S NOT ENOUGH to be baptized in the Holy Spirit one time. You have to stay filled with the Spirit. As Christians, it seems, we spring leaks.

When we read the Book of Acts, we see clearly that the apostles weren't just filled with the Spirit once and for all on the day of Pentecost (Acts 2:4). We also read two more accounts of the disciples being filled with the Spirit in Acts 4:31 and Acts 13:52. If the apostles—who were witnesses of Christ's ministry on earth, death, and resurrection—had to be filled with the Spirit over and over again, how much more so do we?

Ephesians 5:18 says, "Do not be drunk with wine, for that is reckless living. But be filled with the Spirit." The Message paraphrase says, "Drink the Spirit of God, huge draughts of Him." The ISV admonishes us to "keep on being filled with the Spirit." And the Amplified Classic puts it this way: "But ever be filled and stimulated with the [Holy] Spirit." That is accurate since the tense for the Greek word *filled* in Ephesians 5:18 literally means "keep on being filled constantly and continually."[1]

I constantly ask the Lord, "Fill me with Your Spirit." I know I need a fresh infilling. I know a little dab won't do me. I need "huge draughts of Him." I don't need a goose bump. Every day I need the Holy Ghost stimulation the Amplified Classic version promises to stand against the continual warfare.

When the enemy works to bring death and destruction in our lives, we have to remind ourselves that the Spirit who raised Christ from the dead dwells on the inside of us. Then we need to ask Him to fill us again with that life-giving river. When the enemy comes to frustrate God's purposes in our lives, we need to remember the Spirit of grace is resident in us and ask Him for more, more, and more.

By not being ever filled—continuously filled—with the Holy Spirit, we can be tempted to "flesh out." We can be wooed to walk in the flesh instead of in the Spirit. When mega warfare comes against our minds, it's easy enough to binge-watch something on Netflix we have no business watching because we would rather numb our minds than cast down imaginations.

Instead of fleshing out, eating ice cream, pulling the covers over our heads, or hiding in a cave, we need to boldly approach the throne of God and ask for a fresh infilling of the Spirit. We need to stay full of Him, not full of self-pity, pride, guilt, condemnation, shame, discouragement, and other enemy thoughts that can threaten to overwhelm us.

If you've never been filled with the Spirit and you want to be, pray this prayer:

> *Father, I surrender full control of my life to You. I ask You even now to fill me to overflowing with Your Spirit, just as You have promised to do if I ask according to Your will. I ask this in the name of Jesus and believe that You are pouring out Your Spirit upon me right now.*

BREAK WRONG ALIGNMENTS

WHEN YOUR CAR is out of alignment, it pulls to one side or another. You may have to fight to steer it, and it uses more gas than it should. When your car is out of alignment, it also wears out your tires more quickly.

There are spiritual parallels here we shouldn't ignore. Alignments—those people you submit to, run with, or are otherwise in close connection with—affect your life in ways you may not have considered.

When you are out of alignment spiritually, their influence can pull you to the right or to the left when the Lord wants you on a straight and narrow path. You may have to contend to steer your life in the Lord's direction and spend more energy than you should just to walk in the Spirit. Wrong alignments can wear you out.

Likewise, if you are aligned with someone who has a negative mind-set, if affects you. If you are aligned with someone who is handling money improperly, it affects you. Taking this lesson into the realm of spiritual warfare, if you are aligned with someone who is persistently practicing sin, it affects you. When you walk in alignment with someone, you are partaking in the good, the bad, and the ugly, including the warfare.

When I walk closely with someone, I go to battle when they are in a war. I fight and pray as if it was my battle—because in a way it is. You have to make that level of commitment when you run closely with somebody. You can't just bail out.

Joshua aligned with the Gibeonites, who deceived him by pretending to be from a faraway land, looking for protection. (See

Joshua 9.) The result: the Israelites had to go to war to defend them because they had a covenant.

With all that as background, you can see why you don't want to spend your time and energy sowing in a wrong alignment. You don't want to commit to go to war with somebody who's constantly bringing war on themselves for no good reason. I don't want to align myself with people who are bringing unnecessary warfare on themselves because I don't need any more warfare than I already have. You don't either.

What I've also learned is you can have wrong alignments with good people, people who are holy, loving, and on fire for God. But if it's not a God alignment, it's a wrong alignment, and, again, you are engaging in a war that you aren't called to fight.

Put another way, it can be a distraction. Every good thing is not a God thing. God has right alignments—divine connections—for you. If you spend all your energy working with good people without a God-ordained alignment, you could miss the Holy Spirit relationships that move you faster toward your destiny.

Many times you can have wrong alignments and not even know it unless the Lord highlights the issue. If you have constant warfare in your life, look around you. Who are you aligned with? Are they in constant warfare? Break wrong alignments, and the warfare load will lighten.

Spiritual Warfare Tactic 25

CULTIVATE RIGHT ALIGNMENTS

O NCE YOU BREAK wrong alignments, you need to look for and cultivate right alignments. Some of those alignments can be seasonal. Paul and Barnabas had a strong alignment, one that helped Paul find acceptance among the Jews despite his early persecution of Christians, but they eventually separated over a disagreement in ministry.

Paul and Silas also had a strong alignment in the spirit. We know Paul aligned with Luke, the physician, who accompanied him on many ministry journeys and wrote the Book of Acts by inspiration of the Holy Spirit. He even forged alignments with his spiritual sons, Timothy and Titus. Those are just a few of the alignments in Paul's life.

Right alignments, those that are synergistic and help you advance in God, can be beneficial from a spiritual warfare perspective. When I come under heavy fire, I need people I can trust to stand with me. I need people who won't judge me, people I can tell what is really going on in my mind. I need people around me who know how to fight demon powers to war with me. God-sent alignments have tight lips, have your back, and have the integrity not to share your personal life with others or break your boundaries. True friends are consistent and don't merely say the words but do the actions to back them up.

When you cultivate right alignments, you ultimately have less warfare because you're forming a prayer covering over one another to head off the devil at the pass. Right alignments don't eliminate all warfare. The devil will continue raging until the second coming of Jesus.

When you are rightly aligned, though, you have a greater confidence knowing someone has your back and can help you discern the enemy's plots against you. You are standing with someone who will rally the troops on your behalf. You have someone in your corner who can vouch for your character when enemy accusations come.

In 1 Samuel 18–20 Saul tried to kill David a dozen times. Jonathan, Saul's son, had a covenant relationship with David and stood with him through the assaults. Even though Jonathan was next in line for the throne of Israel, he helped David escape his father's wrath. (See 1 Samuel 20.) That's a self-sacrificing friend.

Ecclesiastes 4:9–12 tells us, "Two are better than one, because there is a good reward for their labor together. For if they fall, then one will help up his companion. But woe to him who is alone when he falls and has no one to help him up. Also if two lie down together, then they will keep warm; but how can one keep warm by himself? And if someone might overpower another by himself, two together can withstand him. A threefold cord is not quickly broken."

Godly alignments also unlock wisdom that you may not otherwise have. This is especially strategic in spiritual warfare. Proverbs 11:14 says, "Where there is no counsel, the people fall; but in the multitude of counselors there is safety."

Spiritual Warfare Tactic 26

MEDITATE ON *the* WORD *of* GOD

JOSHUA WAS A fierce warrior in his own right, but he discovered the ultimate success—leading the Israelites into the Promised Land and conquering enemy after enemy after enemy—when he took heed to God's instructions. Indeed, Joshua had an extraordinary track record on the battlefield—he even managed to see the sun stand still in one war—by obeying this command from God:

> Be strong and very courageous, in order to act carefully in accordance with all the law that My servant Moses commanded you. Do not turn aside from it to the right or the left, so that you may succeed wherever you go. This Book of the Law must not depart from your mouth. Meditate on it day and night so that you may act carefully according to all that is written in it. For then you will make your way successful, and you will be wise.
> —JOSHUA 1:7–8

Joshua saw the miracles in Moses's ministry. He sat outside the tent when Moses talked face to face with God. But by following Jehovah's instruction, Joshua did something even Moses didn't do—he saw God's prophetic promise about the land flowing with milk and honey come to pass. Joshua knew the Book of the Law inside and out. He knew the ways of God. He knew the Word of God because he meditated on it.

Meditating on the Word of God will build your faith. Meditating isn't just for the Buddhists or the New Agers. God started the idea.

I love Noah Webster's 1828 Dictionary. Its definitions often offer Scripture. It's worth a look at Webster's classic definition of *meditate*. It means "to dwell on any thing in thought; to contemplate; to study; to turn or revolve any subject in the mind." Webster offers Psalm 1:2 as an example: "His delight is in the law of the Lord, and in His law doth he meditate day and night."[1] In Joshua 1:8 the Hebrew word for meditate (*hagah*) gives us another level of meaning: "to murmur, ponder, imagine, mutter, speak, study, talk, utter."[2] I submit to you that if you murmur, ponder, imagine, speak, and study the Word of God, your faith will act as a shield to block doubt from your mind. (For those of you who are doubting the suggestion, what do you have to lose?)

I can't stress enough how important it is to meditate on the Word of God. Along with praying in tongues, it is vital to your spiritual growth and maturity because you can agree with the Word all day long, but you won't see change in your life until you renew your mind to the truth you say you believe.

When your mind is renewed to the Word in any area, it becomes natural for you to walk in the light that you have. It becomes easier to be a doer of the Word than to walk after the ways of the world. Let Psalm 19:14 be your prayer: "Let the words of my mouth and the meditation of my heart be acceptable in Your sight, O LORD, my strength and my Redeemer."

CONFESS *the* WORD *of* GOD

JESUS IS THE "High Priest of our confession" (Heb. 3:1, NKJV). The word *confession* in that verse has the same etymology as the Greek word *homologeō*, which means "to say the same thing as."[1] We need to say about ourselves and our situations what the High Priest of our confession says about us and our circumstances.

What is Jesus confessing over us? We find His will for our lives in the Word of God. His Word is His will. Jesus is confessing to the Father that we're more than conquerors (Rom. 8:37), that we're covered in the blood (Rev. 1:5), that we're righteous in Him (2 Cor. 5:21), and that we're seated with Him in heavenly places (Eph. 2:6). Jesus is sitting at the right hand of the Father ever making intercession for us (Heb. 7:25).

Make a confession list now before the warfare hits. There is power in the Word of God that you confess over your life. I have a confession list that is about fifteen pages. One list deals with who I am in Christ. The other deals with scriptural promises I'd like to see manifest, things I am believing for.

I can honestly tell you that in just a few short years of confessing the Word over my life, I ended up with major victories, including healing from high blood pressure. I am also debt-free and own four properties. I am doing what I am called to do, and I have much more peace in my life than I once thought possible.

Confessing the Word of God over your life brings results. Stick with it. Victorious Christian living relies on the power in God's Word, not in the power of self. And God's Word is powerful. Consider the Spirit-inspired words from the writer of Hebrews:

For the Word that God speaks is alive and full of power [making it active, operative, energizing, and effective]; it is sharper than any two-edged sword, penetrating to the dividing line of the breath of life (soul) and [the immortal] spirit, and of joints and marrow [of the deepest parts of our nature], exposing and sifting and analyzing and judging the very thoughts and purposes of the heart.

—HEBREWS 4:12, AMPC

Second Timothy 2:15 says, "Study and be eager and do your utmost to present yourself to God approved (tested by trial), a workman who has no cause to be ashamed, correctly analyzing and accurately dividing [rightly handling and skillfully teaching] the Word of Truth" (AMPC). I find it interesting that Paul tells Timothy to analyze the Word of God because the Word of God analyzes us. To me, this signifies a symbiotic relationship between the people of God and the Word of God. *Symbiotic* means "living together in more or less intimate association."[2] Victorious Christian living requires an intimate association with the Word.

We need to analyze the Word and extract the truth we need for our daily lives, moment to moment. The Word analyzes us and shows us, like a mirror, where we need to yield to the grace of God as we become more like Jesus. There's no striving, no struggling, no frustration. There is just an intimate relationship with a loving God whose thoughts are higher than our thoughts and whose ways are higher than our ways (Isa. 55:9). Thank God, He has given us His thoughts and made record of His ways in His Word. It shouldn't be a challenge to delight ourselves in it and say the same thing as Jesus about ourselves and our circumstances.

Spiritual Warfare Tactic 28

RELEASE *the* PRAYER *of* FERVENT FAITH

J AMES, THE APOSTLE of practical faith, speaks of the "prayer of faith" and "fervent prayer" in the same passage. Releasing the prayer of fervent faith is one key to overcoming the fiery darts the enemy releases at you.

> And the prayer of faith will save the sick, and the Lord will raise him up. And if he has committed any sins, he will be forgiven. Confess your faults to one another and pray for one another, that you may be healed. The effective, fervent prayer of a righteous man accomplishes much.
>
> —JAMES 5:15–16

Other translations speak of "the prayer offered in faith" (NIV) and "the earnest (heartfelt, continued) prayer of a righteous man makes tremendous power available [dynamic in its working]" (AMPC).

When it comes to spiritual warfare, you need fervent, earnest, heartfelt, continued prayers of faith. I've learned a fervent spirit is a defense against the devil. In fact, zeal is part of our spiritual armor (Isa. 59:17). Remember, fervency, zeal, and passion run together. Where you find one, you'll find the others.

It's impossible to be fervent without displaying passion. It's impossible to be zealous without a fervent spirit. That's why many in spiritual warfare circles are so animated and loud when they pray. While volume does not equal authority—you can whisper in the name of Jesus and demons must bow—volume often echoes out of a fervent spirit.

God expects you to be fervent. It's a command. It's a theme that runs through the Bible and is especially manifest in the Book of Acts. The Bible specifically talks about fervency in several contexts: being fervent in spirit (Rom. 12:11); being fervent in mind (2 Cor. 7:7); laboring fervently in prayer (Col. 4:12; James 5:16); and loving one another fervently (1 Pet. 1:22; 4:8).

Where you see fervency, you see salvations. Where you see fervency, you see miracles. Where you see fervency, you see deliverance. Where you see fervency, you see the spirit of Christ showing up on the scene to work with those who believe.

Can you imagine? Have you ever watched water boil? It bubbles up with utter intensity, and sometimes it even escapes the confines of the pot. Boiling water can't hide its expression. In fact, if you come too close to a pot of boiling water, the steam alone will get your attention.

Oh, that we saw this fervent spirit in the church more often today rather than the apathetic and lukewarm spirit that allows the flesh, the world, and the devil to have their way. When the Lord returns, will He find fervent faith in the earth (Luke 18:8)?

You must release the prayer of faith in the midst of spiritual warfare and watch God rise up and fight for you or send angel armies to war on your behalf. You must pray in faith to see the mountains of sickness, debt, mind traffic, family strife, or other enemy opposition cast out of your midst. Consider the words of Jesus:

> Have faith in God. For truly I say to you, whoever says to this mountain, "Be removed and be thrown into the sea," and does not doubt in his heart, but believes that what he says will come to pass, he will have whatever he says. Therefore I say to you, whatever things you ask when you pray, believe that you will receive them, and you will have them.
>
> —MARK 11:22–24

BREAK *the* POWERS
of the ENEMY

THE ENEMY HAS a measure of power in the earth. The Bible calls him the god of this world (2 Cor. 4:4), the prince of the power of the air (Eph. 2:2), and the ruler of this world (John 16:11). First John 5:19 (ESV) tells us plainly, "We know that we are from God, and the whole world lies in the power of the evil one."

The good news is the enemy has no authority over us. We are in the world, not of the world (John 17:16). Greater is He who is in us than he who is in the world (1 John 4:4). We have authority to break the powers of the enemy. Jesus Himself said in Luke 10:19 (KJV):

> Behold, I give unto you power to tread on serpents and scorpions, and over all the power of the enemy: and nothing shall by any means hurt you.

God has given us power to combat the devil's power. It's helpful to look at the translation of the Greek words for *power* in this verse. God gave us power (*exousia*) over the power (*dunamis*) of the devil.

One definition of *exousia* is "power of choice, liberty of doing as one pleases."[1] We can choose not to tolerate the wicked one's schemes. We can choose to break the power of the enemy and walk in liberty. *Exousia* also means "physical and mental power; the ability or strength with which one is endued, which he either possesses or exercises."[2] We can choose not to allow the enemy to attack our physical bodies and minds by exercising our power over him.

The Greek word *dunamis* means "strength, power, ability; power consisting in or resting upon armies, forces, and hosts."[3] The *exousia* power of God is no match for the *dunamis* power of the enemy. When we choose to break the powers of the enemy in any area where he seems to be overpowering God's will, in Jesus's name the demonic assignment is broken.

When we break the powers of an enemy attack, the enemy's power can no longer hurt us. The Greek word for hurt is *adikeō*, which means "to act unjustly or wickedly; to have violated laws in some way; to do wrong; to hurt, damage, harm; to wrong someone, act wickedly towards him."[4]

If the enemy is hurting you, understand that he is violating the law. His actions are unjust. Your just God has given you the power to enforce His rule of law in your life. You have a covenant with the Lord God Almighty. You can break the power of the enemy. Rise up and say, "Devil, I break your powers against my life, my family, my business, and my finances in Jesus's name!"

STIR UP *the* GIFT *of* GOD *in* YOU

Have you stirred up your gift lately? The apostle Paul told Timothy to stir up the gift of God—and keep it stirred up. I like how the Amplified Bible, Classic Edition puts it: "Stir up (rekindle the embers of, fan the flame of, and keep burning) the [gracious] gift of God, [the inner fire] that is in you" (2 Tim. 1:6, AMPC). We know that Paul was talking about the gift of the Holy Ghost in this scripture, and it's vital to build yourself up in your most holy faith by praying in the Spirit (Jude 20), but victorious spiritual warfare also means exercising your natural God-given gifts and talents for His glory.

Jesus expects you to use your God-given gifts and talents to advance the kingdom. The kingdom of God suffers violence, and the violent take it by force (Matt. 11:12). When you serve, you are plundering hell's kingdom. But when you serve when all hell is breaking loose against you, you put the enemy on notice that you bow only to Jesus. So when warfare breaks loose against you, don't stop serving; serve all the more. Don't stop giving; give all the more. If you can build a wall, get some bricks and mortar and start building. If you can drive a van, pick up people and take them to church. Get your mind off yourself, trust God, and do good. It's a spiritual warfare tactic that drives the devil mad.

The concept of using your God-given talents to bring kingdom increase is biblical, isn't it? Remember the parable of the talents? In Matthew 25:14–30 Jesus told the story of a man who was about to go on a long journey. He called his servants together and entrusted his possessions to them. To one he gave five talents, to another he gave two talents, and to another he gave one talent. The man who received one talent operated in a spirit of fear. He let warfare against his mind overtake him. His master was not pleased. When you are in a war, don't stop doing what God has called you to do. Do it with all the more passion.

Proverbs 24:10 says, "If you faint in the day of adversity, your strength is small." If the enemy can get you off your post with a flu bug or a teenager's rebellion, he'll keep using that tactic to steal your peace in this realm and your eternal rewards in the next realm.

Take Paul's advice: stir up the gift in you. Beyond the five-fold gifts listed in Ephesians 4 and the gifts of the Spirit listed in 1 Corinthians 12, there are the kingdom gifts listed in Romans 12:3–8, like serving, exhorting, giving, ruling, and showing mercy. You may not feel all that spiritual—spiritual enough to teach or prophesy—when the battle is raging against your mind, but you can still stir yourself up enough to serve.

COME AGAINST
the ENEMY

IN EPHESIANS 6 Paul made it clear we are not wrestling against flesh and blood. Then he used the word *against* over and over again. Let's look at the scripture.

> Put on the whole armor of God that you may be able to stand against the schemes of the devil. For our fight is not against flesh and blood, but *against* principalities, *against* powers, *against* the rulers of the darkness of this world, and *against* spiritual forces of evil in the heavenly places.
> —EPHESIANS 6:11–12, EMPHASIS ADDED

It's helpful in this spiritual warfare context to look at the Greek word for against, which is *pros*. It means "to the advantage of; at, near, or by; to, towards, with, or with regard to."[1]

Wrestling is not a long-distance sport. When we wrestle, we are "near" the enemy and moving "towards" him with an eye toward victory. When we come against principalities, powers, rulers, and spiritual forces, it's a head-on confrontation in which we have the advantage in Christ.

We know the enemy forms weapons he can use against us. Paul calls them fiery arrows (Eph. 6:16). Other translations call them "fiery darts" (KJV), "flaming missiles" (AMPC), "flaming arrows" (NIV), "inflamed darts" (DARBY), or "blazing bolts" (Aramaic New Testament in Plain English). But God's Word promises:

> But no weapon that is formed against you shall prosper, and every tongue that shall rise against you in judgment you shall show to be in the wrong. This [peace, righteousness,

security, triumph over opposition] is the heritage of the servants of the Lord [those in whom the ideal Servant of the Lord is reproduced]; this is the righteousness or the vindication which they obtain from Me [this is that which I impart to them as their justification], says the Lord.

—Isaiah 54:17, ampc

Indeed, when we come against our enemies, we can rest assured God is coming against our enemies. When we stand against them, God stands against them. Consider these promises:

The Lord will cause your enemies who rise up against you to be defeated before you; they will come out against you one way and flee before you seven ways.

—Deuteronomy 28:7

He delivers me from my enemies. You lift me up above those who rise up against me; You have delivered me from the violent man.

—Psalm 18:48

Though I walk in the midst of trouble, You will preserve me; You stretch forth Your hand against the wrath of my enemies, and Your right hand saves me.

—Psalm 138:7

David understood Deuteronomy 20:1: "When you go out to battle against your enemies, and see horses, and chariots, and a people that outnumber you, do not be afraid of them, for the Lord your God is with you, who brought you up out of the land of Egypt." This understanding that when he chooses to come against God's enemies, God will rise up and fight for him fueled his faith to battle the giant Goliath. Listen to David's faith-filled words:

David said to the Philistine, "You come against me with sword and spear and javelin, but I come against you in the

name of the LORD Almighty, the God of the armies of
Israel, whom you have defied."

—1 SAMUEL 17:45, NIV

When you sense the enemy coming against you, don't flee. Come
against the enemy in the name of Jesus and watch him flee instead.

Spiritual Warfare Tactic 32

TAKE AUTHORITY OVER *the* ENEMY

JESUS BOLDLY CLAIMED, "All authority has been given to Me in heaven and on earth" (Matt. 28:18). The Greek word for authority in that verse is *exousia*. In addition to the definitions of *exousia* we uncovered in the tactic "Break the Powers of the Enemy," *exousia* also means "the power of rule or government (the power of him whose will and commands must be submitted to by others and obeyed."[1] That sums up Christ's authority.

Jesus gave His disciples a measure of His own authority, jurisdiction, influence, and anointing so they could go about doing good and healing all who were oppressed by the devil (Acts 10:38). In Matthew 10:1 we read the account of Jesus commissioning His disciples to move in the gifts of the Spirit: "He called His twelve disciples to Him and gave them authority over unclean spirits, to cast them out, and to heal all kinds of sickness and all kinds of disease."

Like the disciples, God has authorized you to stand against the enemy. *Merriam-Webster* offers the world's definition of *authority*: "power to influence or command thought, opinion, or behavior."[2] But *exousia* is more than that; it includes the concept of "authorization."[3]

Authority is the power to act on God's Word. When God speaks, you are authorized to move. When you are authorized, you are commissioned, certified, licensed, lawful, legitimate, recognized, sanctioned, warranted, and official. Jesus delegated His authority in His name. *HELPS Word-Studies* reveals *exousia* "('delegated power') refers to the authority God gives to His saints—authorizing them to act to the extent they are guided by faith (His revealed word)."[4]

You exercise your authority by faith, not by feelings. The authority to demand the devil loose what belongs to you is yours, whether you feel like you've got it or not. You can feel powerless, but the truth is you have power and authority. Authority has nothing to do with emotions. But you must exercise it for it to be effective.

Jesus has already done everything He's going to do about the devil. He's already done everything He's going to do about sickness. It's up to you to do something now. He is waiting on you to use the authority He gave you to manifest the kingdom of God in your life.

Now here's the catch in spiritual warfare: you need to be under authority to have authority. In other words, you need to submit to God's authority in order to successfully exercise Christ's delegated authority. Jesus Himself said, "I did not come of My own authority, but He sent Me" (John 8:42). You are not sent forth into battle in your own authority. You must get instructions from God, who sends you into battle with His authority.

When He sends you into battle, you have the permission and privilege to exercise His authority in His name. You can simply declare, "I take authority over (fill in the blank, whether it's sickness, pain, confusion, or some other enemy assignment) in Jesus's name." When you believe you have authority and have faith in the One who delegated it, you will see results. It's important that you meditate on the authority you have because, like a dog, the enemy can sense when you are walking by fear instead of by faith.

DON'T BREAK RANK
and ISOLATE YOURSELF

T HE ENEMY WANTS you to break rank and isolate yourself from those who would otherwise war for you and with you. That's one of the worst things you can do in the heat of the battle because that's when the enemy turns up the fire seven times.

If the wicked one can convince you to take on an offense that separates you from those who would typically stand with you, he can work overtime on your mind, will, and emotions and wreak all the more havoc in your life.

The American Heritage Dictionary of Idioms defines *break ranks* this way: "fall out of line or into disorder; also, fail to conform, deviate."[1] *Cambridge Dictionary of American Idioms* explains the military meaning: "to walk away from a straight row in which you and other soldiers have been standing."[2]

In a military sense ranks are the members of an armed service—the enlisted personnel, not the officers. This sense of the word carries over into the body of Christ. In the Lord's army, in some cases the ranks have been wounded by the officers leading them, sending them into a battle they weren't trained well enough to fight or throwing them in the line of fire to protect themselves. In other cases ranks have wounded themselves by not following orders or have been hit with friendly fire from others in God's army who were careless or disobedient.

Whatever the case, it's not wise to break rank. David's mighty men did not break rank. Gideon's army did not break rank. As a soldier in the army of the Lord, you must not break rank. You must remain loyal to the captain of the Lord's host. If you've been wounded by friendly fire in battle, forgive those who hurt you and let the Lord heal you so you can take your rightful place in the company of warriors and counsel, where there is safety (Prov. 11:14).

Isolating yourself is one degree beyond breaking rank. You can choose not to fight in God's army but still be among God's people. But when you isolate yourself from fellowship with the saints, you are setting yourself up for enemy attack. When you refuse to reach out for help but would rather quarantine yourself from your local church, refusing to answer your phone when the pastor calls, you are not walking in God's wisdom.

Consider the words of Solomon: "Whoever isolates himself seeks his own desire; he breaks out against all sound judgment" (Prov. 18:1, ESV). Isolation is actually a selfish act that defies common sense. Don't allow demonic imaginations to paint your friends as your enemies. Even if they have caused you harm, they are not your ultimate enemy, and God calls us to walk in forgiveness. Unforgiveness opens a door wide for enemy intrusion.

If you've been oppressed by the enemy and are fearful of returning to the front lines, take counsel with wise warriors who can take authority in prayer over the enemy's assignment against your life, help you discover new spiritual warfare technologies, and stand with you in warfare. God needs you at your post.

Spiritual Warfare Tactic 34

PRAY *for* REVELATION *of the* ROOT

WHEN WARFARE IS hitting your life, you don't want to take a buckshot approach in the battle. Rather, you want to lay an ax to the root of the issue. That means discerning the root.

I've learned that if you pick a fight with a devil that's not picking a fight with you, you've got two devils to fight instead of one. In other words, if you don't discern accurately what is coming against you and start calling out various spirits in your binding and loosing exercise, you are just stirring up devils that didn't have you on their radar screen.

You need to know what is hitting you so you can intentionally hit it back. Paul put it this way: "So, therefore, I run, not with uncertainty. So I fight, not as one who beats the air" (1 Cor. 9:26). The New Living Translation says, "I am not just shadowboxing." You don't want to swing wildly, hoping to hit something in the realm of the spirit.

Again, you need to discern the root of your opposition. Sometimes you may think you're being opposed by the enemy when you're really being opposed by God. Twice the Holy Spirit prevented Paul from going into a territory to preach the gospel. Other times Satan hindered him. Here are three questions that may help to discern where the opposition is coming from.

1. **Ask the Holy Spirit what is going on.** First of all you need to pray and ask the Lord what is going on. When in doubt, your best first move is to trust in the Lord and not on your own understanding. Just because you have seen a pattern in how Satan works doesn't mean

you can automatically presume what spirit is behind something. Ask the Lord what spirit is operating.

2. **Did God already tell you to do it?** If you are convinced the Holy Spirit expressly told you to do something and you are meeting with obstacles, it's likely the enemy is trying to prevent fruit for the kingdom. Satan constantly works to hinder God's plan even though he is already defeated.

3. **What's going through your mind?** The Word says you should think on good things (Phil. 4:8). If the hindrance you face is coming in the form of unpleasant thoughts and fearful imaginations, that's not God speaking to you. It is the devil's way to get you into fear, doubt, and unbelief.

Learn to discern the different voices whispering in your ear during times of warfare. One way to get to the root of a demonic voice is to consider your emotions. If you are feeling depressed, a spirit of heaviness is one probable root. If you are feeling afraid, it's the voice of fear. If you are feeling like giving up, it could be the voice of discouragement. You can't resist what you don't discern, but once you can see it, you can defeat it.

Remember, you are not wrestling against flesh and blood, but you are wrestling. The key is to wrestle with the enemy and not with God. In other words, you don't want to be resisting God when you should be resisting the enemy, and you don't want to be cooperating with the enemy when you should be cooperating with God.

Spiritual Warfare Tactic 35

CONSUME SPIRITUAL WARFARE TEACHING

Consuming spiritual warfare teaching and reading spiritual warfare books is a practical technique to reinforce what you may know but sometimes forget when the battle is raging. Studying what the Word of God has to say about warfare and gleaning from the experiences of others who have gone before you could open your eyes to what you are facing in the spiritual realm.

Of course, not all spiritual warfare teaching and books are in line with Scripture, so you need to be careful who you listen to and what you read. But there are some time-tested teachers from today and decades ago who have solid truth on spiritual warfare. What took them years or decades to discover can be passed on to you, at least in part, in a teaching series or a book.

Look for spiritual warfare teachers who rely heavily on the Word. The Bible says, "All Scripture is inspired by God and is profitable for teaching, for reproof, for correction, and for instruction in righteousness, that the man of God may be complete, thoroughly equipped for every good work" (2 Tim. 3:16–17). And 2 Timothy 2:15 says, "Study to show yourself approved by God, a workman who need not be ashamed, rightly dividing the word of truth."

When I am going through a battle, I listen to and read time-tested spiritual warfare teachers to help me gird up the loins of my mind. "Faith comes by hearing, and hearing by the word of God" (Rom. 10:17). So when the teachers and authors use Scripture, it helps build my faith for the battle.

Testimonies also build my faith for the battle and help me realize that I am not alone in the fight. Through the testimonies of those who have overcome in spiritual warfare—and the nitty-gritty details they share about the fierce battle they endured—I am reminded of this Scripture:

> No temptation has taken you except what is common to man. God is faithful, and He will not permit you to be tempted above what you can endure, but will with the temptation also make a way to escape, that you may be able to bear it.
>
> —1 Corinthians 10:13

If you are getting attacked in your physical body, consume teaching on healing. If you are getting attacked in your marriage, listen to messages that encourage your faith in that area. If you are fighting for your prodigals, read stories of those who saw dramatic turnarounds and find out how they prayed.

Don't rest on your laurels in warfare. Feed your spirit. The enemy is working to wear you down. You need a continual stream of meat from the Word to chew on. You can even go to sleep listening to the Bible—your spirit doesn't sleep—or to a teacher breaking down the Word in ways you can digest it, even when you are fighting for your life.

ASK *the* HOLY SPIRIT
to LEAD YOU *in* BATTLE

In THE REALM of the spirit there are principalities, powers, rulers of darkness, and spiritual wickedness (Eph. 6:12). But there is also the Holy Spirit—and the Spirit of God is more powerful than the spirit of the world, the spirit of fear, the spirit of sabotage, or any other spirit that orchestrates an attack against our lives.

The Holy Spirit is the third person of the Godhead, coequal with the Father and the Son (Acts 5:3–4). He is the co-Creator of the universe (Gen. 1:1–3) and the author of Scripture (2 Tim. 3:16). He is omnipresent (Ps. 139:7–10), omniscient (1 Cor. 2:9–11), and omnipotent, just as the other two persons of the Godhead are (Luke 1:35; Rom. 15:19). He is the one who overshadowed Mary and caused her to conceive Jesus in human form (Matt. 1:18; Luke 1:35), and He will glorify Christ forever (John 16:13–14).

The Holy Spirit is our strongest ally in any war we face as we walk the earth. When He ascended to heaven, Jesus sent the Holy Spirit to be our Helper, our Teacher, our Comforter, our Advocate, our Intercessor, our Strengthener, the One who empowers us, the Revealer of truth, and our Standby. (See John 14–16, AMPC.) The Holy Spirit leads us (Rom. 8:14); guides us into truth and shows us things to come (John 16:13); prays through us (Rom. 8:26); endues us with Christ's power (Acts 1:8); and much more.

Part of the "much more" is leading us into battle. See, we're not called to fight every battle and every war. The battle ultimately belongs to the Lord, and if He needs our help, He will lead us to the battle line. Sometimes we engage in other people's battles and wind up unleashing hell in our own lives. I'm not saying we shouldn't pray for and with those who are under fire. I am saying we need to allow the Holy Spirit to lead us into battle just as we allow Him to lead us in every other area of our lives.

Second Corinthians 2:14 assures us, "Now thanks be to God who always causes us to triumph in Christ." When we follow the Holy Spirit into battle and do things His way, He will lead us into triumph as super-conquerors for God's glory. If we lead ourselves into battle, we might lead ourselves into the wrong battle, at the wrong time, in the wrong way.

"Shall I go up?" (2 Sam. 5:19). David, a mighty warrior for God, asked Jehovah this critical question before running to the battle line—and we would be wise to do the same.

Although we war from a place of victory, rushing into spiritual warfare outside God's timing can lead to defeat. Although we are taught to remain on the offensive, entering a battle God has not called us to fight can be a dangerous mistake. And although we're in a spiritual war, the battle really is the Lord's.

We need to be led by the Holy Spirit into battle if we want God to lead us into triumph. If we lose a battle, it could very well be that the Holy Spirit didn't lead us into the spiritual skirmish in the first place.

ASK *the* HOLY SPIRIT
WHAT WEAPON *to* USE

JUST AS A surgeon uses different equipment for different procedures and a golfer uses different clubs in different areas of the green, spiritual warriors need to ask the Holy Spirit what weapon or weapons to use in each individual battle. You may find yourself in a battle similar to one you fought and won in a past season, but that's no guarantee that the same weapon will take out the demon you are fighting now.

Sure, there are baseline strategies and weapons that you must always employ and deploy. You can't go into battle without your armor on and without the name of Jesus on your lips. But if you want to be ultra-effective in warfare, you need to use the right weapon. Using the wrong weapon is like trying to cut down a tree with a butter knife. You might eventually get the tree to fall, but it will take you much longer and wear you out in the process. The Holy Spirit knows what weapon will bring you the fastest victory.

Second Corinthians 10:4 tells us, "For the weapons of our warfare are not carnal, but mighty through God for the pulling down of strongholds." The Greek word for weapons in that verse is *hoplon*. It means "any tool or implement for preparing a thing; arms used in warfare, weapons; an instrument."[1] The Greek word for warfare is *strateia*, which is defined as "an expedition, campaign, military service, warfare."[2]

What are the weapons of our warfare? The weapons are different than the whole armor of God, though there is some crossover: the sword of the Spirit (the Word of God), prayer, praise, worship, the anointing on our lives to break yokes, and the blood of Jesus.

The Holy Spirit showed me that we already possess every weapon we need for battle, but we sometimes don't know we have them. He showed me that the fruit of the Spirit manifested can be a weapon against the enemy: love, joy, peace, patience, gentleness, goodness, faith, meekness, and self-control (Gal. 5:22–23). It drives the devil crazy when we walk in love or remain at peace. It's one way we submit ourselves to God, resist the devil, and watch him flee (James 4:7).

Rest assured, there is a right weapon for your expedition—and you are equipped for battle. Second Peter 1:3 makes it clear: "His divine power has given to us all things that pertain to life and godliness through the knowledge of Him who has called us by His own glory and excellence." When the Holy Spirit shows you what weapon to use, you can be confident you have the weapon at your disposal and He will help you to wield it.

Before you enter the battlefield, pray this prayer:

> *Father, I thank You that You have called me to walk in victory in every area of my life. I discern the enemy at hand. Help me choose the right weapon to see the swiftest victory for Your glory. Teach me to discern the proper artillery to carry into this battle, in Jesus's name.*

BREAK
DEMONIC CYCLES

Have you ever felt like you are living in a vicious circle? Even now you may be trying your best to solve a problem only to discover that every step you take is making the problem worse—or even creating new problems.

If that's you, stop and ask yourself: Is this a vicious circle or a demonic cycle? In other words, is one trouble in your life leading to another because of the classic law of cause and effect, a law that can easily snowball for better or worse? Or are you wrestling against principalities and powers, against the rulers of the darkness of this world, and against spiritual wickedness in high places (Eph. 6:12)?

Demonic cycles—a phrase I use to describe how demons create and manipulate strongholds in our minds to tempt us to walk around the same mountain over and over again—are real. Demonic cycles are more than just bad habits, and demonic cycles can be more difficult to break because you may not even recognize there's a mental stronghold involved in your drama. And you can't break the power of something you don't know is there.

Demonic cycles could manifest as overeating, job instability, yearly sickness, relationship issues, problems with authority, and many other undesirable woes. Demons can whisper in your ear and fortify ungodly thoughts in any area of your mind that isn't renewed.

With demonic cycles, spirits often work to perpetuate acts of self-sabotage of which you are unaware. You start a new job, but you have the same personality that conflicts with the boss you encountered at the last job. You get a new boyfriend and soon enough end up having the same arguments you had with the last boyfriend. You plan to get up an hour earlier to read your Bible and pray, but you end up getting distracted by less-than-eternal purposes. So you find yourself looking for a new job and a new boyfriend even as you are dying on the vine because you aren't feeding your spirit. The common denominator is you. Whether you know it or not, you are allowing the demonic cycle to continue. Are you beginning to see it?

Breaking the power of vicious circles is often a matter of making better choices, but when it's a demonic cycle, you need to identify the imaginations and wrong thought patterns that are allowing wicked spirits to wreak havoc on your life. Ultimately you have to take responsibility for your choices. No demon in hell is stronger than a will aligned with the Word of God. God's grace floods the soul that seeks first the kingdom of God and His righteousness (Matt. 6:33).

The apostle Paul offers some good advice: "For though we walk in the flesh, we do not war according to the flesh. For the weapons of our warfare are not carnal but mighty in God for pulling down strongholds, casting down arguments and every high thing that exalts itself against the knowledge of God, bringing every thought into captivity to the obedience of Christ, and being ready to punish all disobedience when your obedience is fulfilled" (2 Cor. 10:3–6, NKJV).

In order to break demonic cycles rooted in soulish strongholds, you have to make a purposeful and diligent effort to cast down the imaginations that defy the Word of God. As a believer, you have the privilege of using God's Word to tear down barriers erected against His truth. You have the power to fit every loose thought and emotion and impulse into the structure of a life shaped by Christ. Your tools are ready at hand for clearing the ground of every obstruction and building lives of obedience into maturity.

RUN *to the* BATTLE LINE

Run to the battle line. Run to the war. Don't run away from the fight; run into it. It's been said there's a reason why our armor doesn't cover our backs—because we're to face demon powers toe-to-toe rather than fleeing in fear.

When it comes to David's famed battle against Goliath, we see him running to the battle three times. The first run was when his father, Jesse, told him to carry food to his brothers at the battle line. When he arrived on the scene, he heard the war cry. "David left his things with the keeper of the equipment, and he ran to the battle line" (1 Sam. 17:22). David's first instinct when he heard the war cry was to run to the battle line. He did not shrink back in fear even though he wasn't trained or armed. He ran toward the skirmish.

After seeing the Israelites shaking with fear, David volunteered to fight the giant Goliath one-on-one, face-to-face, toe-to-toe. He didn't ask for time to pray about it. He didn't ask to go home and kiss his parents good-bye. He could have gone back to tending the sheep, but he answered the call of God to rise up and fight a battle that others were too scared to tackle.

David ran to the battle line for a second time, this time drawing even closer to the enemy. He moved so fast he didn't have time to think twice. In other words, he didn't give the devil time to talk him out of the fight. First Samuel 17:48 tells us: "When the Philistine arose and came near to meet David, David hurried and ran toward the battle line to meet the Philistine." He was in a hurry to do God's will.

The third time David ran was to finish off the enemy. First Samuel 17:50–51 concludes: "David prevailed over the Philistine with a sling and with a stone. And he struck down the Philistine and slew him, but there was no sword in the hand of David. Therefore David ran and stood over the Philistine. Then he took his sword and drew it from out of its sheath, and he finished him off and he cut off his head with it. When the Philistines saw their champion was dead, they fled."

David didn't walk. He ran. He didn't jog. He ran. The Hebrew word for ran in 1 Samuel 17:51 is *ruwts*. It means "to run swiftly, dart; move quickly." It also means "to drive away from, cause to run away."[1] David ran to the battle line. The enemy ran from the battle line. David claimed the victory.

The lesson: don't shrink back from the conflict. You can't win if you don't fight, but if you run to the battle line understanding God has your back, He will never let you fall.

BREAK EVERY YOKE

THE ENEMY WORKS to put yokes upon our necks to oppress us. What is a yoke? Naturally speaking and in this context, it's "an arched device...laid on the neck of a defeated person."[1]

When a yoke is upon you, it causes you to hang your head down low. God is in the yoke-breaking business. He once told the Israelites, "I am the LORD your God, who brought you out of the land of Egypt, that you should not be their slaves, and I have broken the bars of your yoke and made you walk upright" (Lev. 26:13).

There are many types of yokes. There are yokes of depression, yokes of financial debt, yokes of fear, yokes of sickness, and so on. Anything that is oppressing you or holding you in bondage—lying on your neck and causing you to walk in defeat—qualifies as a yoke. Thankfully Jesus came to set the captives free by breaking oppressive yokes. In fact, in Matthew 11:28–30, He said:

> Come to Me, all you who labor and are heavily burdened, and I will give you rest. Take My yoke upon you, and learn from Me. For I am meek and lowly in heart, and you will find rest for your souls. For My yoke is easy, and My burden is light.

The Amplified Classic translation of Matthew 11:30 says, "For My yoke is wholesome (useful, good—not harsh, hard, sharp, or pressing, but comfortable, gracious, and pleasant), and My burden is light and easy to be borne."

You are Christ's servant and willingly take on His yoke, but

He has not called you to labor and be heavily burdened by the enemy's yoke. Thankfully, you have the power of the Holy Spirit— the anointing—to break every yoke that is not of God. Isaiah 10:27 assures us, "The yoke shall be destroyed because of the anointing oil."

The anointing breaks the yoke. The anointing abides in you (1 John 2:27). That means you can rise up in the power of God and break every yoke the enemy has put upon you. You can declare emphatically, "I break this demonic yoke off my neck by the anointing of God that abides in me. I break this yoke of (fill in the blank) right now, in Jesus's name. I will not walk in oppression, bondage, or defeat. I reject this yoke. I take on the yoke of the Lord Jesus Christ, which is light and easy to be borne."

Going back to the lesson on alignments, yoking yourself with unbelievers can also bring an oppressive force upon you. That's why the Bible tells us, "Do not be unequally yoked together with unbelievers. For what fellowship has righteousness with unrighteousness? What communion has light with darkness?" (2 Cor. 6:14).

BREAK *the* STRANGLEHOLD *of* WORRY

Y OU ARE CALLED to fight the good fight of faith (1 Tim. 6:12). But your adversary the devil roams around like a roaring lion, intent on devouring your faith (1 Pet. 5:8). One way the devil does this is by trying to choke you, or put you in a stranglehold. In the wrestling world—and remember, you are wresting against principalities, powers, rulers of the darkness of this world, and spiritual wickedness in high places, according to Ephesians 6:12—a stranglehold is an illegal hold that chokes the opponent. *Merriam-Webster* calls it "a force or influence that chokes or suppresses freedom of movement or expression."[1] If the wrestler doesn't break free from the stranglehold, the lack of blood or air can cause him to black out.

Translating this to spiritual realities, the enemy wants to choke the Word of God out of your mouth so you can't wield your sword of the Spirit or pray. The enemy wants to choke your revelation of who you are in Christ. The enemy wants to choke your understanding of your authority over him. The enemy wants to counter the work of the blood of Jesus and the Holy Spirit in your life so you'll sideline yourself. You need to learn how to prevent the enemy from getting you into a stranglehold in the first place—but if you've fallen into the devil's trap, you can break free with one simple prayer.

What is this stranglehold I'm talking about? Worry. Did you know that the definitions of *worry* include "to harass by tearing, biting, or snapping especially at the throat," "to shake or pull at with the teeth," and "to assail with rough or aggressive attack or treatment"?[2]

This is one of the enemy's so-called roaring lion tactics. He magnifies your circumstances to get you to worry. Once you begin to worry, he moves in position to engage you in a stranglehold that makes you feel powerless to do anything about what has you worried. It's a clever strategy that plays on internal cares that you haven't cast on the Lord or that you continue taking back from His able hands.

Jesus warns us repeatedly not to worry, but He also tells us what to do instead. He inspires our faith for provision by telling us to look at nature and assuring us of our value to Him. Then He instructs us to get our mind off what we need—and that could be anything, from provision to healing to protection to relationship-mending and beyond—and seek the kingdom of God and His righteousness (Matt. 6:25–34).

If you've already fallen into the enemy's trap, you can do what Peter suggested before he warned us to be vigilant "because your adversary the devil walks around as a roaring lion, seeking whom he may devour" (1 Pet. 5:8): You can cast all your worry on Him, because He cares for you (v. 7). And when you feel that anxiety and worry rising up in your soul, you can take Paul's advice:

> Be anxious for nothing, but in everything by prayer and supplication, with thanksgiving, let your requests be made known to God; and the peace of God, which surpasses all understanding, will guard your hearts and minds through Christ Jesus.
>
> —Philippians 4:6–7, NKJV

When you do these things, the enemy can't keep his grip on you. Amen.

Spiritual Warfare Tactic 42

BREAK DECEPTION
OFF YOUR MIND

WARNINGS OF DECEPTION are peppered throughout the Bible. In fact, almost every book in the New Testament has some warning about deception or deceivers. Jesus said, "Take heed that no one deceives you" (Matt. 24:4) and "Beware lest you be deceived" (Luke 21:8). Paul warned, "Let no one deceive himself" (1 Cor. 3:18) and "Do not be deceived" (1 Cor. 6:9). I could go on and on with these warnings from Scripture. The devil is a deceiver (Rev. 12:9). He's a liar and the father of lies (John 8:44).

The Bible says, "The heart is deceitful above all things, and desperately wicked" (Jer. 17:9, NKJV). If that's true, and it is, then none of us are above deception. If we think we are, then we're deceived already. But the good news is Jesus sent the Holy Ghost to lead and guide us into all truth (John 16:13), truth that is readily confirmed in the canon of Scripture. If we follow His Spirit and His written Word instead of the idolatry of our hearts, we'll walk in the light.

Truth is a weapon of our warfare, but when we don't walk in the truth or when we've been taught a lie or believed an error, deception can settle in our souls. One deception can leave the door open to another deception. The Bible says, "A little leaven leavens the whole lump" (Gal. 5:9, NKJV). The Message paraphrase puts it this way: "It only takes a minute amount of yeast, you know, to permeate an entire loaf of bread."

Still, as Walter Kambulow notes, "We can't blame all this deception business on the devil. Nor can we be ignorant to his devices. Part of his ministry is to find the idolatry in our hearts:

the deceitfulness of riches, the pride of life, the lust of the flesh, or something else that causes us to give God's place to another. Once Satan finds that idolatry he'll tempt you with it. At that point we have a clear choice: destroy the idol or walk into darkness."[1]

The other side is discernment. The reality is many have simply not been activated or trained to discern spirits. Yet discernment is a vital gift in this hour as false prophets, false teachers, and even false christs are rising around the world with smooth sayings, rhymes, and riddles. At its most basic level, *discern* simply means to show insight and understanding. Some have a discerning eye for art. Others have a discerning palate for food. We need to develop a discerning spirit that safeguards us from deception in this hour. The Bible commands us not to be deceived.

The nature of deception is you don't know you are deceived. Continually renewing your mind with the Word of God will break off deception, but it doesn't happen overnight. When you find yourself in a raging war and know your mind is running away with you, your emotions are taking you on a roller coaster, and your will is bowing to the flesh, take the opportunity to break deception off your mind because you are believing something that is not true. Just say, "Lord, if there is any deception on my mind, break it off, in Jesus's name. Shine the light of Your truth in my soul and deliver me from deception."

Spiritual Warfare Tactic 43

CALL YOUR INTERCESSORS

As PRAYER WARRIORS, we like to quote Ephesians 6:11–18. But that is not where Paul the apostle stopped. He had another weapon against the wiles of the wicked one. He had reinforcements who were making intercession for him in Jerusalem, in all Judea and Samaria, and to the end of the earth. He didn't just hope they might pray when the Holy Spirit brought him to mind; he petitioned for their prayers.

Once we get past the whole armor of God and personal prayer challenge, we see Paul the apostle reaching out for spiritual warriors to join his intercessory prayer team: "Pray for me, that the power to speak may be given to me, that I may open my mouth boldly to make known the mystery of the gospel, for which I am an ambassador in chains, that I may speak boldly as I ought to speak" (Eph. 6:19–20).

Of course, we know that Paul returned the favor and prayed for his spiritual sons, co-laborers, churches, and even his enemies. Prayer is a partnership. We should all pray for one another. Whether we're soccer moms, business executives, students, or in full-time ministry, we all need intercessors in our lives to help us in the midst of our fiercest battles. While it's our responsibility to lift up the shield of faith, sometimes the onslaught against us seems broader than a single shield can protect against. We all need what the late C. Peter Wagner called a "prayer shield" in times of intense warfare.[1]

Everyone should have two or three people with whom they walk closely enough to share personal struggles and battles for the purpose of prayer. If you are walking through serious health issues, for example, it's not always wisdom to let everyone know. Well-meaning people tend to share bad news with anyone and everyone, which can release more warfare against you as people speak the power of death over your life.

At the same time, certain personal struggles in the realm of temptation are highly confidential and private. You don't need to confess everything to the church when you are ready to quit, working your way out of a pit, or otherwise stumbling into the enemy's snare of sin. Having two or three intercessors who know how to pray without judging can help you gain victory over battles you can't or shouldn't fight alone.

Beyond this intimate group, you can build a network of another ten who know more than the general public but not as much as your core team. On a broader scale you can join intercessory prayer groups in your church or even online in which many stand together and fight together in an offensive position. In other words, you are pushing back darkness before it manifests—and if it does manifest, you are corporately taking authority over it.

Whatever kind of prayer support you can muster, remember it won't do you much good if you don't rally the troops when you are in a war. Although some intercessors will pick up on what you are going through and reach out to let you know what they see and hear—and what they are praying—others won't know you need help if you don't release a cry for help. Call your intercessors in early and often!

BREAK GENERATIONAL CURSES

SOMETIMES THE PRESENCE of a generational curse will leave an open door for constant enemy attack. A generational curse is iniquity that was passed to you from the generations in your bloodline who walked before you.

It's absolutely true that "Christ has redeemed us from the curse of the law by being made a curse for us—as it is written, 'Cursed is everyone who hangs on a tree'—so that the blessing of Abraham might come on the Gentiles through Jesus Christ, that we might receive the promise of the Spirit through faith" (Gal. 3:13–14). Still, generational curses must be broken in the name of Jesus. Two scriptures reveal the reality of generational curses:

> You shall not bow down to them or serve them; for I, the LORD your God, am a jealous God, visiting the iniquity of the fathers on the children to the third and fourth generation of them who hate Me.
>
> —EXODUS 20:5

> The LORD is slow to anger and abounding in mercy, forgiving iniquity and transgression; but He will by no means clear the guilty, visiting the iniquity of the fathers upon the children to the third and fourth generation.
>
> —NUMBERS 14:18

Generational curses can manifest in key areas of your life as weaknesses, defeat, poverty, failure, sickness and disease, barrenness, humiliation, and helplessness. Your ancestors may have opened the door to such curses through stealing, lying, disloyalty, dishonoring their parents, anti-Semitism, idolatry, stinginess toward God, various forms of sexual immorality, acting unjustly toward the poor, making false covenants, depending on the arm of the flesh instead of on God, cursing themselves, or curses from witches or those who had authority over you.

You may notice a curse that manifests as cancer in the bloodline. You may have a curse of divorce or abandonment or other family strife issues in your family generations. Being accident prone or a history of premature, unnatural deaths or suicides could indicate a generational curse is present. Reproductive problems, whether among males or females, is a sign of a curse in the family line. Mental disease can also fall under this category. The key, again, is looking at your family history. Doctors may not know it, but when they ask for your medical history and probe with questions about disease in your family history, they are essentially pinpointing a possible generational curse.

In order to break a generational curse, you must first identify it. If you notice patterns of sin in your life that you cannot seem to break no matter how much time you spend with God, how much deliverance you go through, or how much you resist the devil, there could be a curse at work. You may notice people in your family have the same iniquities working in their lives.

Once you identify the curse, you can repent for your sin and the sin of your ancestors. You also need to forgive the past generations. At that point, you can break the curse by the power of the blood and in the name of Jesus. Rise up and decree and declare the curse is broken and ask the Lord for His blessing on your life and on your family.

WAIT UPON
the LORD

WAITING ON THE Lord is strategic for two reasons: First, we must wait for His unction and His battle plans to enter the fight. Second, once we get in the raging battle, we may find ourselves growing weary and being tempted to give in to the battle against our mind, the pressure the enemy puts on our tongues to speak out his plans, and the exhaustion of our flesh. Even still, while we're fighting, we need to keep the Lord's perspective.

But the instruction to wait upon the Lord comes with a brilliant promise that encourages my heart every time I read it. We find this promise in Isaiah 40:29–31. I like the Amplified Classic version of this scripture because it draws out the Hebrew:

> He gives power to the faint and weary, and to him who has no might He increases strength [causing it to multiply and making it to abound]. Even youths shall faint and be weary, and [selected] young men shall feebly stumble and fall exhausted; but those who wait for the Lord [who expect, look for, and hope in Him] shall change and renew their strength and power; they shall lift their wings and mount up [close to God] as eagles [mount up to the sun]; they shall run and not be weary, they shall walk and not faint or become tired.

The renewing of strength is an awesome promise in the middle of the battle. The guarantee of not growing weary and fainting? I'll take that one too. But I wanted to point your attention to the other part of this verse: "They shall mount up with wings as eagles"

(v. 31). Eagles can soar to heights of over ten thousand feet. The eagle can see at least twice as far as a human. And eagles are symbolic of prophetic ministry.

When you want a prophetic perspective—God's perspective—on anything from your daily trials to your future decisions, wait on the Lord. Expect Him. Look for Him. Hope in Him. He will cause you to soar above the storms in your life as an eagle soars above the clouds in the sky.

When you wait upon the Lord, you get a bird's-eye view. He will give you a prophetic perspective on your situation so you can see the proverbial forest instead of getting overwhelmed by the trees. You see things from ten thousand feet, so to speak. Waiting on the Lord may make you feel as if you are sitting and doing nothing. You may be sitting still, but you aren't doing nothing. The Bible says, "Be still and know that I am God" (Ps. 46:10).

I like how The Message puts Isaiah 40:28–31: "He doesn't get tired out, doesn't pause to catch his breath. And he knows everything, inside and out. He energizes those who get tired, gives fresh strength to dropouts. For even young people tire and drop out, young folk in their prime stumble and fall. But those who wait upon God get fresh strength. They spread their wings and soar like eagles, they run and don't get tired, they walk and don't lag behind."

Spiritual Warfare Tactic 46

PRAY *the*
APOSTOLIC PRAYERS

P RAYING THE APOSTOLIC prayers is a strategic way to gird
yourself up for battle or stay strong in the midst of even the fiercest
warfare. The apostolic prayers are intercessory petitions Paul the
apostle made in his various epistles, as well as some prayers we find
in the Book of Acts. Pray these prayers in the first person; make
them your personal prayers.

Pray:

> *God of our Lord Jesus Christ, the Father of glory, give me
> the Spirit of wisdom and revelation in the knowledge of
> You, that the eyes of my understanding may be enlightened,
> that I may know what is the hope of Your calling and
> what are the riches of the glory of Your inheritance among
> the saints, and what is the surpassing greatness of Your
> power toward us who believe, according to the working of
> Your mighty power, which You performed in Christ when
> You raised Him from the dead and seated Him at Your
> own right hand in the heavenly places, far above all prin-
> cipalities, and power, and might, and dominion, and every
> name that is named, not only in this age but also in that
> which is to come. And You put all things in subjection
> under His feet and made Him the head over all things for
> the church, which is His body, the fullness of Him who fills
> all things in all ways (Eph. 1:17–22).*

Give me, according to the riches of Your glory, power to be strengthened by Your Spirit in the inner man, and that Christ may dwell in my heart through faith; that I, being rooted and grounded in love, may be able to comprehend with all saints what is the breadth and length and depth and height, and to know the love of Christ which surpasses knowledge; that I may be filled with all the fullness of God (Eph. 3:16–19).

∾

Now, Lord, look on their threats and grant that I, Your servant, may speak Your word with great boldness, by stretching out Your hand to heal and that signs and wonders may be performed in the name of Your holy Son, Jesus (Acts 4:29–30).

∾

I pray that my love may abound yet more and more in knowledge and in all discernment, that I may approve things that are excellent so that I may be pure and blameless for the day of Christ, being filled with the fruit of righteousness, which comes through Jesus Christ, for the glory and praise of God (Phil. 1:9–11).

∾

I ask that I may be filled with the knowledge of Your will in all wisdom and spiritual understanding; that I may walk in a manner worthy of the Lord, pleasing to all, being fruitful in every good work, and increasing in the knowledge of You, strengthened with all might according to Your glorious power, enduring everything with perseverance and patience joyfully, giving thanks to You, who has enabled me to be a partaker in the inheritance of the saints in light (Col. 1:9–12).

You can also create first person prayers from the following scriptures: Romans 15:13; 1 Thessalonians 5:23; 2 Thessalonians 1:11–12; and 2 Thessalonians 3:1–5.

BLESS YOUR ENEMIES

Blessing your enemies is a biblical command—and it's also a stealth warfare strategy. I'm not talking about blessing devils, mind you. I am talking about blessing the people who have given themselves over to the enemy's destructive agenda.

Jesus taught, "You have heard that it was said, 'You shall love your neighbor and hate your enemy.' But I say to you, love your enemies, bless those who curse you, do good to those who hate you, and pray for those who spitefully use you and persecute you, that you may be sons of your Father who is in heaven. For He makes His sun rise on the evil and on the good and sends rain on the just and on the unjust" (Matt. 5:43–45).

Peter taught, "Do not repay evil for evil, or curse for curse, but on the contrary, bless, knowing that to this you are called, so that you may receive a blessing" (1 Pet. 3:9). Paul taught this principle: "Beloved, do not avenge yourselves, but rather give place to God's wrath, for it is written: 'Vengeance is Mine. I will repay,' says the Lord. Therefore 'If your enemy is hungry, feed him; if he is thirsty, give him a drink; for in doing so you will heap coals of fire on his head'" (Rom. 12:19–20).

Now, Paul wasn't talking about heaping coals of judgment on their head but coals of conviction. When you return good for evil, you set the stage for God to soften someone's heart toward you. When you pray for those who spitefully use you and curse you, many times the first thing God will bless them with is a revelation that they are in the wrong.

You can bless your enemies with kind words. You can always

find something positive to say about people, even mean-spirited people, because they are created in the image of God. Maybe they have a strong work ethic you can praise. Maybe they have a strong fashion sense you admire.

You can send them gifts. That would fall into the "do good to them" category. Send them a gift card to a department store or send them a kind greeting card. This will disarm them. You can speak well of them in public, or at least refuse to speak ill of them. When you speak well of your enemies in public, it gets back to them in private.

Beyond that, intercede as the Holy Spirit leads you until you feel a release in your spirit. And remember, Paul admonishes you to "bless those who persecute you; bless and do not curse" (Rom. 12:14). At the root, *bless* means "to speak well of," and *curse* means "to speak ill of." So don't respond to your persecutors by running all over town telling people what they did to you. If you do, you'll be guilty of gossip, slander, and cursing your enemy. Move in the opposite spirit. If you respond God's way, you'll be blessed.

As for your enemy, well, he's likely to be blessed with some conviction from the Holy Spirit, and your prayers pave the way for you both to grow in the character of Christ as you guard your heart from bitterness. Amen.

Spiritual Warfare Tactic 48

SUBMIT YOURSELF
to GOD

Y OU'VE PROBABLY HEARD James 4:7 plenty of times, or at least part of it. James, the apostle of practical faith, wrote: "Therefore submit yourselves to God. Resist the devil, and he will flee from you." We're quick to quote the second half of this verse—the resisting the devil part. But we need to put at least as much emphasis on the first half of this verse. In fact, we'd do well to look at the full context of this Spirit-inspired statement, which runs from James 4:6–10:

> But He gives more grace. For this reason it says: "God resists the proud, but gives grace to the humble." Therefore submit yourselves to God. Resist the devil, and he will flee from you. Draw near to God, and He will draw near to you. Cleanse your hands, you sinners, and purify your hearts, you double-minded. Grieve and mourn and weep. Let your laughter be turned to mourning, and your joy to dejection. Humble yourselves in the sight of the Lord, and He will lift you up.

When we resist God instead of resisting the devil, we're showing a lack of submission that is rooted in pride. Pride is the sin that sparked Lucifer's great fall from heaven. When we submit ourselves to God, we find more grace to war—and we need grace. Drawing near to God in the face of enemy attack shows a humble heart of dependence and submission. We need to humble ourselves under His hand, repenting for any areas of our lives that we haven't submitted to Him, and He will lift us up above our enemies. He will even prepare a table before us in the presence of our enemies on the day of vindication (Ps. 23:5).

Submitting ourselves to God sometimes means submitting ourselves to one another out of a reverence for Christ (Eph. 5:21); submitting ourselves to elders (1 Pet. 5:5); or submitting ourselves to our leaders (Heb. 13:17). We need to maintain an attitude of submission to God at all times, but much more so when we see enemy fire coming into our camp! We need to walk a finer line when the battle is raging. Romans 8:7 tells us our carnal mind does not and cannot submit to the laws of God. Galatians 5:17 reveals the flesh wars against the Spirit and the Spirit against the flesh. We need to crucify our fleshly responses to spiritual warfare so we are warring with the Spirit instead of against the Spirit.

Proverbs 3:5–6 exhorts us to "Trust in the LORD with all your heart, and lean not on your own understanding; in all your ways acknowledge Him, and He will direct your paths." Acknowledging the Lord is vital at all times, yet how much more so in wartime! If we want Him to direct our paths around the enemy's land mines, we need to submit ourselves to His leading, not running out ahead of Him in misplaced zeal or lagging behind Him in fear. If we want to wear God's armor and use His mighty weapons to pull down strongholds and exercise the authority He delegated to us in His name, we need to submit ourselves to God.

RESIST
the DEVIL

JAMES 4:7 IS a one-two punch against the demon that's punching you. Again, the verse reads: "Therefore submit yourselves to God. Resist the devil, and he will flee from you."

That word *resist* is from the Greek word *anthistémi*, which means to "take a complete stand against, a contrary position; to establish one's position publicly by conspicuously holding one's ground; refusing to be moved."[1] Once we have submitted to God, we are in a far better position to resist the devil because there's a stronger grace on us to stand and withstand. Put another way, it's difficult to resist the devil when we aren't submitted to God because we have common ground with the enemy in the area of our disobedience.

First John 3:8 says plainly, "Whoever practices sin is of the devil, for the devil has been sinning from the beginning. For this purpose the Son of God was revealed, that He might destroy the works of the devil." When we are practicing sin, we are not submitted to our holy God. It's one thing to sin and repent. It's another thing altogether to practice sin.

When we submit ourselves to God, we can resist the devil. So how, practically speaking, do we resist the devil? We resist the devil when we stand on the Word of God, which is immovable and incorruptible. God's Word is the rock on which we stand. Since resisting the devil often means resisting his lies, we must stand on the truth in God's Word, thinking about it and talking about what God says of a situation rather than what the devil is whispering in our ears.

We resist the devil by resisting the temptation to sin, running to the battle line, and casting down vain imaginations. We resist the devil by keeping on our armor, walking in the Spirit, staying watchful and prayerful, and wielding the weapons of our warfare. We see many of these tactics outlined in this book.

So why, then, when we are resisting the devil, does it seem the enemy doesn't flee? I know "God is not a man, that He should lie" (Num. 23:19). The Word is absolutely 100 percent true all the time, without fail. And God's Word says every knee must bow to the name of Jesus (Phil. 2:10). So what gives?

When God's Word doesn't seem to be working, this I know: it's not God's Word that's not working. Usually we're either missing some revelation or doing something wrong somewhere, whether we realize it or not. Either way, we need a revelation!

Sometimes I really do think there's just an onslaught of demons that come one after another. We command one to flee, and there's another right there to take its place. But I do know this: if we worship God in the midst of the battle, He will war against our enemies. So while we shouldn't hesitate to go on the offensive against our enemies with revelation from the Holy Spirit, I believe worshipping God generates the intimacy with His heart, the faith in His name, and the humility we need to remain victorious in warfare no matter how many devils come rushing our way.

Spiritual Warfare Tactic 50

SOW
a SEED

Sowing a seed can break a cycle of spiritual warfare in your life. In the parable of the sower Jesus spoke of a farmer who was sowing seed. Some of the seed fell beside the path, some on rocky ground, and some among thorns. Only the seed that fell on good ground produced a harvest. (See Matthew 13:1–9, 18–23.)

The Word of God is seed in your life, but the enemy works to rob you of that seed by sowing tares in your soul. Put another way, most of the time Satan gains entrance into your mind by sowing a seed in the form of a lie.

Jesus explains that when you don't understand His Word or when you aren't rooted or when you worry or chase money, the seed does not bear fruit. The enemy sows seeds of doubt as to whether or not God's Word is true. He sows fearful or greedy thoughts to drive you to take faithless actions that cause a crop failure. This is one of the devil's warfare devices of which Paul warns not to be ignorant (2 Cor. 2:11).

While you must continually sow the Word of God into your soul to renew your mind as a combative tactic against the enemy's slick moves to steal, kill, and destroy your harvest with his deceptive seeds, sometimes you need to sow other seeds in the natural to break a cycle of war in a certain area of your life. If your relationships are under attack, sow a seed. If your health is targeted, sow a seed. If your finances are in distress, sow a seed. If you have a prodigal whom you are believing God will bring home, sow a seed.

There are many types of seeds you can sow. Prayer is the first seed we should always sow, but in prayer God may give you a sowing strategy to break the devil's back. For example, God may tell you to sow a kind word. He may tell you to sow a gift. He may tell you to sow a certain amount of money into a ministry.

When the enemy is working to bring division in any area of your life—dividing you from friends or family, dividing you from health and well-being, dividing you from your dream—one of the best ways to multiply your firepower is to sow a financial seed. Jesus said you'll put your treasure where your heart is (Matt. 6:21). If the enemy is working to divide you from something close to your heart, sow a seed to break the devil's back and believe for a harvest of God's intervention.

When you are under a financial attack, you should definitely sow a financial seed. The enemy wants you to pull back and clam up and hold your seed out of fear. That's the perfect time to sow a sacrificial seed, displaying your utter trust in God as your provider.

When you sow, name your seed and sow in faith and tell the devil, "You aren't stealing my harvest." Galatians 6:7 assures us, "Be not deceived. God is not mocked. For whatever a man sows, that will he also reap."

Spiritual Warfare Tactic 51

AVOID JOB'S JUDGMENTAL FRIENDS

UNFORTUNATELY EVERYONE SEEMS to have friends who like to judge us when life isn't going our way. At times the enemy uses those close to you to add fuel to his fiery darts when what you really need is someone to stand in the gap for you. Here's a strategy: avoid Job's judgmental friends.

Job's judgmental friends offered him plenty of reasons to feel guilty and condemned. His wife went so far as to tell him to "curse God and die" (Job 2:9). Now, don't turn in the same spirit and judge your friends for being judgmental and unsupportive. That won't help you in the battle either.

Sometimes there's really no way anyone can understand your pain. Often friends and family try to sympathize but really can't empathize. They don't have any idea what it is like to walk in your shoes. They can't see things from your perspective. They aren't enduring the battle coming against your mind. They just don't get it.

When you are going through trials, facing serious battles, or otherwise struggling, the best thing to do is to be slow to speak (James 1:19). After all, the Bible says there is a time to keep silent and a time to speak (Eccles. 3:7). If you are surrounded with friends like those of Job, Negative Nancys, and Debbie Downers, sharing your heart is not going to help you and may hurt you.

Job's judgmental friends kick you when you are down. The Bible says, "Do not withhold good from those to whom it is due, when it is in the power of your hand to do it" (Prov. 3:27). Many times, when we're going through a trial, we need kindness. Kindness is a fruit of the Spirit, and any friend operating in the fruit of the Spirit will show you kindness in a time of need. Job's judgmental friends won't offer genuine kindness. Job 6:14 puts it this way: "A despairing man should be shown kindness from his friend, or he forsakes the fear of the Almighty."

Job's judgmental friends bring guilt and condemnation and insist you have open doors to the enemy. We should all examine our hearts when the onslaught comes to make sure we don't have any open doors. And Proverbs 25:11–12 says, "The right word at the right time is like a custom-made piece of jewelry, and a wise friend's timely reprimand is like a gold ring slipped on your finger" (THE MESSAGE).

However, Job's judgmental friends give pat answers and platitudes that do not reflect God's heart in the midst of our battle. Let's face it, pat Bible answers—"cast all your cares" and "those whom He loves He disciplines"—that really don't apply to your situation are anything but a word in due season.

Take the time when you are not in battle to determine whom you can talk to during times of intense spiritual warfare and trials. Discern those who will lean into the Spirit and let Him inspire their words and actions. Who will stand with you and proclaim the opposite of what you see and hear coming against you, share a prophetic word that edifies, comforts, and exhorts, or just keep their mouths shut altogether and just be with you? Find those friends. Avoid Job's judgmental friends, and if you can't avoid them, pray for them.

Spiritual Warfare Tactic 52

NEVER LET *the* DEVIL
SEE YOU SWEAT

PAUL THE APOSTLE offers some especially strategic advice for battle in his epistle to the church at Philippi: "And do not [for a moment] be frightened or intimidated in anything by your opponents and adversaries, for such [constancy and fearlessness] will be a clear sign (proof and seal) to them of [their impending] destruction, but [a sure token and evidence] of your deliverance and salvation, and that from God" (Phil. 1:28, AMPC).

In other words, never let the devil see you sweat, but keep praising God because He has it under control. I like the CEV version of this verse also: "Be brave when you face your enemies. Your courage will show them that they are going to be destroyed, and it will show you that you will be saved. God will make all of this happen."

Who are your enemies? Not people; not really. The devil is your enemy. He sometimes uses people to hurt you, but the origin of evil is the devil. If your best friend betrays you, don't show the devil you are disappointed. Pray for those who spitefully use you. If you can't pay your rent, don't stress over your finances. Your God shall supply all your needs according to His riches in glory by Christ Jesus (Phil. 4:19). If the doctor gives you a bad report, don't speak death over your life. God's name is Jehovah Rapha, the Lord who heals you (Exod. 15:26). If you just feel like giving up, don't voice your resignation. Jesus will never leave you or forsake you (Heb. 13:5). He'll never give up on you. If you don't quit, you always win.

Don't let the devil see you sweat. That doesn't give glory to God. Think about it for a minute. Was Jesus ever for a moment frightened or intimidated in anything by His opponents and adversaries? No, He wasn't. If you are born again, you are in Christ and you have no reason to fear anything or anyone. When a trial comes in your life, the devil is watching and God is watching. Who's going to get the glory? If you get worried and scared, you are giving the devil glory. If you stand in faith, with nothing wavering, you are giving God the glory.

When you let the devil see you sweat, so to speak, you are demonstrating that you have more fear of the devil than respect for the Lord. When you start talking about all your problems and walking in worry, you are demonstrating that you have more faith in what the devil is showing you than faith in what the Lord has told you. When you let the devil see you sweat, you are not in complete unity with God because you are not walking in His Word.

So how do you keep from caving in under the enemy's pressure? How do you stand firm in faith when all hell is breaking loose against you? The concept is simple: look at things from God's perspective and pray. What is God's perspective? God's perspective is in His Word. God doesn't break a sweat when you can't pay a bill. God doesn't start biting His nails when you lose your job. God doesn't have a nervous breakdown when you get a bad report. No, God laughs at the enemy because He knows the end of your story. You win if you stand in faith!

RENEW YOUR MIND
in the AREA *of* ATTACK

PAUL EXHORTS IN Romans 12:2, "Do not be conformed to this age, but be transformed by the renewing of your mind, that you may prove what is the good and acceptable and complete will of God." The AMPC version really draws out the deeper intent of Paul's wise words:

> Do not be conformed to this world (this age), [fashioned after and adapted to its external, superficial customs], but be transformed (changed) by the [entire] renewal of your mind [by its new ideals and its new attitude], so that you may prove [for yourselves] what is the good and acceptable and perfect will of God, even the thing which is good and acceptable and perfect [in His sight for you].

The word *renew* in this scripture comes from the Greek word *anakainōsis*, which is defined as "a renewal, renovation, complete change for the better."[1]

Again in Ephesians 4:23 Paul says, "Be renewed in the spirit of your mind." The AMPC tells us to "be constantly renewed in the spirit of your mind [having a fresh mental and spiritual attitude]." And the NLT puts it this way: "Let the Spirit renew your thoughts and attitudes."

There is a war going on to renew your mind. The enemy wants to conform you to the world's way of thinking. He wants to renovate your belief system with dark lies so he can change your life for the worse. He wants you to adapt your thought process to his deceptive agenda. God wants you to renew your mind and attitude toward spiritual warfare so you can enforce His perfect will in your life.

It's up to you to renew your mind. When the enemy is attacking your mind with wily whispers, you need to renew your mind in the area of the attack. For example, if your body is hit with sickness, it's not the time to study prosperity. It's time to renew your mind to the reality that God is your Healer; when you were saved, you were healed; and if you were healed, then you are healed. If you are getting smacked with a financial attack, it's not the time to do an in-depth study on angels. You need to renew your mind in the area of provision and prosperity.

When you realize that there's a certain weakness, you shore up that weakness. If you have a leak in the roof of your house, you don't install new bathrooms. You fix the roof. As believers, sometimes we study what we feel like studying instead of what we need to study. We chase various revelations at times rather than renewing our minds in the area where we need the most edifying.

Consider in any given battle where you are really seeing attacks, whether it's in just one area or multiple areas. Discern the thoughts associated with the battle. Then find scriptures you can study that will renew your mind in that weak spot the enemy is attacking.

Remember, when you set out to renew your mind, you are submitting yourself to God's thoughts. And God's thoughts toward you are peaceful and hopeful: "For I know the thoughts that I think toward you, saith the Lord, thoughts of peace, and not of evil, to give you an expected end" (Jer. 29:11, KJV).

Spiritual Warfare Tactic 54

REMEMBER *the* BATTLE
IS *the* LORD'S

WHEN THE ENEMY is attacking, we take it personally, especially when he's attacking our characters, our bodies, our finances, and our families. What we have to ultimately remember amid the barrage of thoughts raging against our minds and the feelings swelling up in our souls is that the battle really isn't ours. The battle belongs to the Lord—and the Lord never loses a battle.

When we were born again, we were automatically enlisted as soldiers in the army of God. We were given military garb—the armor of God. We were given an arsenal—the weapons of our warfare, which are not carnal but mighty in God for the pulling down of strongholds (2 Cor. 10:4). And we were given a dossier on the enemy.

The enemy is attacking us because we are on God's side. He hates us because he hates God. He's not really attacking us; he's attacking the God in us. He wants to kill us, steal from us, and destroy our dreams because we were created in God's image and likeness. Really, it's nothing personal against us. He persecutes us with pleasure to defy our heavenly Father's will in our lives. I like to tell demons that attack me, "My Daddy can beat up your daddy."

Twice in Scripture we see the Holy Spirit, the author of the Bible, sharing through inspired men that the battle is the Lord's. Second Chronicles 20:15 tells us, "Thus says the LORD to you, 'Do not fear, nor be dismayed because of this great army, for the battle is not yours, but God's.'" And 1 Samuel 17:47 assures us, "And then all this assembly will know that it is not by sword and spear that the LORD saves. For the battle belongs to the LORD, and He will give you into our hands."

Our God is a champion. He is the captain of the Lord's host. Exodus 15:3 describes him this way: "The LORD is a man of war; the LORD is His name." He doesn't have a nervous breakdown, flesh out, or hide in a cave when the enemy attacks. Psalm 2:4 says, "He who sits in the heavens laughs; the LORD ridicules them." And Psalm 37:12–13 reveals, "The wicked plot against the righteous, and grind their teeth against them. The Lord will laugh at him, for He sees that his day is coming."

All that is true, and we need to remember it. What is also true is we are Christ's ambassadors on the earth. We are ministers of reconciliation. Jesus told us to occupy until He comes back. He's given us authority and dominion. We are His hands and feet in the earth. In Jeremiah 51:20 God says: "You are My battle-ax and weapon of war: for with you I will break in pieces the nations, and with you I will destroy kingdoms."

The bottom line: the Lord has already defeated the devil, but there's still this battle in the earth realm for the souls. The enemy doesn't want you to rise up and do what you're called to do because he doesn't want you to win souls. But this battle we fight, it belongs to the Lord. When you understand that, you'll also get a revelation that the God who laughs at His enemies will never let you lose a battle He tells you to fight.

REFUSE *to* FOLLOW YOUR EMOTIONS

Y OU ARE AN emotional being. God gave you emotions, and God Himself has emotions. Your emotions can be a great motivator at times and a great enemy at other times.

Think about it for a minute. Sometimes you feel joyful; sometimes you grieve. Sometimes you feel bold, sometimes intimidated. Sometimes you feel triumphant, sometimes completely and utterly physically and emotionally exhausted. Nevertheless, you cannot, you must not, allow your emotions to lead you.

Paul exhorts: "For as many as are led by the Spirit of God, these are the sons of God" (Rom. 8:14). You are a spirit, you have a soul, and you live in a body (1 Thess. 5:23). Your soul is made up of your mind, will, and emotions. Your will is the place within you from which you express your desire, settle on decisions, and drive actions in your life. Your mind is home to your reasoning and intellect.

Your emotions are the seat within your soul that filters events and circumstances through a state of feeling and reacts accordingly. The enemy may work to get you to reason yourself out of God's promises, but he works overtime on emotions to trick you into walking by sight instead of by faith. What you see with your eyes can impact your emotions and hinder your faith.

Your emotions must be submitted to the leadership of the Holy Spirit. Again, the sons of God, the mature in Christ, are led by the Spirit of God. In fact, Watchman Nee, author of books such as *Spiritual Discernment, Secrets to Spiritual Power,* and *Let Us Pray,* once said that emotions are the believer's number one enemy—not the devil, but your emotions.[1] That's why you need to give Him the reins.

If you give God the reins of your heart, you will find stability, but you have to give Him full control of the reins or you are in danger of pulling in the wrong direction in the heat of the battle. If you pick and choose which emotions you will submit to God and which ones you will allow free reign in your soul, you'll wind up unstable—and wound up. You will find yourself holding on tight as the emotional roller coaster turns you upside down and leaves you spinning in circles.

You need to align your emotions with the Word of God. Yes, I know. That's easier said than done. But if David did it, so can you. It's not a matter of putting on a soldier face and keeping a stiff upper lip. David poured out his emotions to God—the anger, the disappointment, the hurt, the confusion—but he did not wallow in those emotions. He submitted them to the one who could stabilize his soul.

A soulish life is dangerous, but if you give God the reins of your heart, you will mature, and you can use your emotions to glorify Him rather than allowing them to lead you away from your purpose in Him. David put it this way, "I will bless the LORD, who hath given me counsel; my reins also instruct me in the night seasons. I have set the LORD always before me: because he is at my right hand, I shall not be moved" (Ps. 16:7–8, KJV). Amen.

Spiritual Warfare Tactic 56

REJECT *the* TEMPTATION *to* FLESH OUT *in* FRUSTRATION

HOW SPIRITUAL DO you become during the midst of your frustrations? Are you spiritually minded when the war is raging, or you do pitch a hissy fit? Do you begin to think, speak, and act out of impatience when the battle hits your mind? Do you keep your sights set on the things of the Spirit when demon spirits are raging against you, or do you rage against your family? What about when sickness or disease knocks on your door? Do you get frustrated? Do you start packing away food when the enemy is piling it on?

Whether it's a minor nuisance or a major aggravation, we've all experienced the opportunity to walk in the Spirit when our flesh is screaming in frustration. We are all familiar with the temptation to allow our flesh to fully manifest our feelings of discontentment. But consider for a moment that frustration is destructive and wastes precious time that could otherwise be used in constructively battling the enemy.

The enemy's overarching purpose with frustrating you is to hinder the grace—the power of the Holy Spirit—to resist him. Few things hinder the grace of God more than frustration. Frustration is not faith. The apostle Paul understood this. In his letter to the Galatians he explained, "I am crucified with Christ: nevertheless I live; yet not I, but Christ liveth in me: and the life which I now live in the flesh I live by the faith of the Son of God, who loved me, and gave himself for me. I do not frustrate the grace of God" (Gal. 2:20–21, KJV).

The enemy wants you to get into the flesh so you will feel guilty, ashamed, and condemned when you finally calm down and see things from God's perspective. The enemy knows if he can get you in a state of condemnation, you won't feel worthy to take your Christ-delegated authority over him.

Consider what happened to Moses when his frustration with the Israelites got the best of him. He rebelled against God and struck the rock twice. The consequence was severe. God forbid him to enter the Promised Land. Could it be possible that faithless acts motivated by your own frustration can keep you from winning your spiritual battles?

The Bible is full of promises that fulfill your needs. If His grace was sufficient for the apostle Paul to endure the satanic messenger that was harassing him, then it's sufficient for you to deal with the satanic messengers that harass you. But here's the key: you need to ask for the grace. When you are tempted to flesh out, you need to draw upon the fruit of self-control, grab hold of yourself, and pray.

Jesus told His disciples not to let their hearts be troubled, distressed, or agitated (John 14:1). That means you have a choice about whether you think, act, and speak in the power of the Spirit and receive grace, or in the frustration of the flesh and receive high blood pressure, migraines, and ulcers. So I set this day before you grace or frustration. Choose grace.

Spiritual Warfare Tactic 57

WALK *by* FAITH
and NOT *by* SIGHT

GOD HAS GIVEN us the measure of faith, and He expects us to walk in it (Rom. 12:3). Paul stated matter-of-factly in 2 Corinthians 5:7, "For we walk by faith, not by sight." It wasn't a command or a suggestion. It was a statement of truth. The AMPC translation really draws out the deeper meaning of Paul's words:

> For we walk by faith [we regulate our lives and conduct ourselves by our conviction or belief respecting man's relationship to God and divine things, with trust and holy fervor; thus we walk] not by sight or appearance.

In the realm of spiritual warfare the enemy is doing everything he can to get us to regulate our lives and conduct ourselves by fear, doubt, and unbelief. He uses what we can see with our eyes to inject double-mindedness into our souls because he knows James 1:6–8 (AMPC) is true:

> Only it must be in faith that he asks with no wavering (no hesitating, no doubting). For the one who wavers (hesitates, doubts) is like the billowing surge out at sea that is blown hither and thither and tossed by the wind. For truly, let not such a person imagine that he will receive anything [he asks for] from the Lord, [for being as he is] a man of two minds (hesitating, dubious, irresolute), [he is] unstable and unreliable and uncertain about everything [he thinks, feels, decides].

The enemy is a master of smoke and mirrors. He is an expert at making mountains out of molehills. The enemy magnifies situations and circumstances in our minds so that they overshadow God's Word in our hearts. The more we focus on what the enemy is showing us—the more we walk by sight—the faster he can dilute our faith.

We know that without faith it is impossible to please God (Heb. 11:6). Jesus assures us we'll receive whatever we ask for in prayer if we have faith (Matt. 21:22). Our faith doesn't rest in our own wisdom, our own intellect, our own genius; it rests in the power of God (1 Cor. 2:5). Scripture tells us God "is able to do exceedingly abundantly beyond all that we ask or imagine, according to the power that works in us" (Eph. 3:20).

Although it's been said seeing is believing, that is not how things work in the kingdom. We don't walk by sight; we walk by faith. The NLT version of 2 Corinthians 5:7 reiterates: "For we live by believing and not by seeing." Hebrews 11:1 tells us, "Faith is the substance of things hoped for, the evidence of things not seen." Indeed, faith doesn't come by seeing; it comes by hearing. Romans 10:17 makes it clear: "So then faith comes by hearing, and hearing by the word of God."

All things are possible if we believe (Mark 9:23). We have to fight the good fight of faith (2 Tim. 4:7). That means refusing to meditate on what the devil throws in our faces or the lies he whispers in our ears. It means keeping the promise set before us, keeping our eyes on the prize. If we are going to walk by sight, then we must walk with Jesus as the center of our focus and watch our faith rise!

Spiritual Warfare Tactic 58

SET *a* GUARD
OVER YOUR MOUTH

THE ENEMY LOVES to put pressure on your tongue. He wants you to boil over like a teapot on a stove and start whistling his tune for your life—but he's always out of tune with God. When that pressure comes—and sometimes it takes the form of people asking you about "how things are going" in any given battle—it's wisdom to set a guard over your mouth. Proverbs 16:23 tells us, "The heart of the wise teaches his mouth."

We see time and time again warnings in Scripture about being careful about what comes out of our mouths. We know the power of death and life are in the tongue, and the devil comes for God's Word in our heart and encourages the words of our mouth that disagree with His plans in a moment of weakness. We need to take these Word warnings seriously:

+ "Let the words of my mouth and the meditation of my heart be acceptable in Your sight, O LORD, my strength and my Redeemer" (Ps. 19:14).

+ "Out of the abundance of the heart the mouth speaks" (Matt. 12:34). If you have fear or doubt in your heart, it will come out of your mouth and the enemy will pounce on the opportunity.

+ "Set a guard, O LORD, over my mouth; keep watch over the door of my lips" (Ps. 141:3). Your mouth is like a door, deciding at some level what comes in and out of your life. When the enemy puts pressure on your tongue, he's looking for an open door. Keep your mouth shut if you can't speak the Word of God.

+ "If I do not remember you, let my tongue stick to the roof of my mouth" (Ps. 137:6). If you can't remember what the Word says, just don't say anything. Sing praises to His name. Pray in the Spirit.

+ "Let no unwholesome word proceed out of your mouth, but only that which is good for building up, that it may give grace to the listeners" (Eph. 4:29). If the words of your mouth don't edify your spirit, if they offer an evil report of your circumstances, ask the Holy Spirit to help you tame your tongue.

+ "That which goes into the mouth does not defile a man, but that which comes out of the mouth, this defiles a man" (Matt. 15:11). The words that come out of your mouth can delay your blessings and defile your future.

The Bible has a lot more to say about the mouth. Essentially, the enemy uses your mouth to trap you. Proverbs 18:21 says, "Death and life are in the power of the tongue, and those who love it will eat its fruit." Proverbs 6:2 says, "You are snared by the words of your mouth; you are taken by the words of your mouth" (NKJV). Proverbs 12:14 says, "A man will be satisfied with good by the fruit of his mouth." And Proverbs 13:3 says, "He who guards his mouth preserves his life, but he who opens wide his lips shall have destruction."

Remember, the devil is after your confession. The pressure on your tongue is meant to tempt you to agree with him so he can use your own power against you. Bite your tongue if you have to, but set a guard over your mouth.

Spiritual Warfare Tactic 59

PRAY *for* WISDOM
in the BATTLE

W E NEED THE Lord's wisdom in the heat of the battle, especially when we're dealing with flesh and blood under demonic influence. When the enemy uses our friends and family—or even natural enemies—against us, we need God's wisdom to separate the personality from the principality, so to speak. We need wisdom to navigate natural relationships that the enemy is working through.

We could all take a hint from Solomon. You know the story. The Lord appealed to Solomon in a dream and made this invitation: "Ask! What shall I give you?" (1 Kings 3:5, NKJV). Can you imagine the Lord coming to you in a dream and making such an invitation? What would you ask God for if you could ask and assuredly receive anything?

It seems Solomon already had enough wisdom to ask for the principal thing: wisdom. Solomon replied to God's invitation with these words: "Give to Your servant an understanding heart to judge Your people, that I may discern between good and evil. For who is able to judge this great people of Yours?" (1 Kings 3:9, NKJV).

That made God happy. Let's see how He responded:

> Because you have asked this thing, and have not asked long life for yourself, nor have asked riches for yourself, nor have asked the life of your enemies, but have asked for yourself understanding to discern justice, behold, I have done according to your words; see, I have given you a wise and understanding heart, so that there has not been anyone like you before you, nor shall any like you arise after you.

And I have also given you what you have not asked: both riches and honor, so that there shall not be anyone like you among the kings all your days. So if you walk in My ways, to keep My statutes and My commandments, as your father David walked, then I will lengthen your days.

—1 Kings 3:11–14, nkjv

God is no respecter of persons (Acts 10:34). You can receive the wisdom you need to wage war against your enemies. James clearly stated, "If any of you lacks wisdom, let him ask of God, who gives to all men liberally and without criticism, and it will be given to him" (James 1:5). The only catch is you have to ask in faith, without doubting. That's not much of a catch, and it shouldn't be too hard to do. God wants to give you wisdom so you can walk wisely, making the best use of your time because the days are evil (Eph. 5:15–17).

God wants to help you win your battles. He has the wisdom you need to put you over the top and launch you into victory. Many times we rely on our own understanding instead of waiting on God's wisdom and make the situation worse.

Wisdom begets wisdom. "The ear of the wise seeks knowledge" (Prov. 18:15). "A wise man listens to advice" (Prov. 12:15, esv). "A man's wisdom makes his face shine" (Eccles. 8:1). "By wisdom a house is built" (Prov. 24:3, niv). Wise ones are cautious and turn away from evil (Prov. 14:16). The words of the wise win him favor (Eccles. 10:12). "The wise will inherit honor" (Prov. 3:35, hcsb). Wisdom will keep and guard you if you love it (Prov. 4:6). I could go on and on. I encourage you to do a study of the benefits of walking in God's wisdom, and when you are in the heat of battle, pray for wisdom, knowing that God will give it to you liberally and without reproach.

Spiritual Warfare Tactic 60

SHUT YOUR EARS *to the* ACCUSER *of the* BRETHREN

Satan is an accuser. He accuses you before God. He accuses you before other people. He accuses God to you. Accusations find their origin in the father of lies, Satan (John 8:44).

John gives an account of a dramatic scene concerning Satan in the Book of Revelation: "Then I heard a loud voice saying in heaven: 'Now salvation, and strength, and the kingdom of our God, and the power of His Christ have come, for the accuser of our brethren, who accused them before our God day and night, has been cast down'" (Rev. 12:10, NKJV).

Here we see that one of Satan's names is the accuser of the brethren. We must shut our ears to his accusations against God and against ourselves. Yes, Satan will accuse you in the midst of warfare with condemning thoughts, thoughts of inadequacy, and other thoughts that work to rob your joy, which is where your strength comes from (Neh. 8:10).

We also must shut our ears to his accusations against others. Satan is a master at the blame game. He'll have you angry with anybody and everybody whom you think isn't standing with you. He'll put the trap of offense in front of you to tempt you into unforgiveness, knowing that resentment dilutes your ability to hear and exercise your authority over his schemes.

You may hear thoughts such as "If she had just answered my call, I wouldn't be dealing with this problem right now" or "If he hadn't told my friend what I said, I wouldn't be on the outside." You may even hear thoughts such as "If God really loved me, He wouldn't allow this to happen."

Sometimes the warfare against you is actually slanderous accusations from the enemy manifesting through the words of others against you. You have to silence your ears to that as well. *Slander* means "to make a false spoken statement that causes people to have a bad opinion of someone."[1] It means to defame, malign, vilify, and asperse, which is a fancy word for a continued attack on one's reputation.

When the accuser of the brethren unleashes slander attacks against you, take heart in this passage from the Sermon on the Mount: "Blessed are you when men revile you and persecute you, and say all kinds of evil against you falsely for My sake. Rejoice and be very glad, because great is your reward in heaven, for in this manner they persecuted the prophets who were before you" (Matt. 5:11–12).

How you respond to mistreatment is one of the most important aspects of your spiritual life. When you respond the right way, you climb higher—or go deeper—in the Spirit. By contrast, when you respond the wrong way, you get bitter. Over time that bitterness will defile your spirit and dull your ability to sense the presence of God or hear His voice.

God is the judge. He will make the wrong things right in His way and in His timing. Vengeance is His. He will repay (Rom. 12:19). I won't be overcome with evil, but I will overcome evil with good (v. 21). I will rejoice when I am persecuted because I know that when I respond the right way, I am blessed. My first response is to pray for those who persecute me. And pray. And pray. And pray some more. It keeps my heart clean. I encourage you to do the same.

Spiritual Warfare Tactic 61

DON'T BLAME GOD
for the WARFARE

SATAN IS SOMETIMES called the accuser of the brethren (Rev. 12:10), but I've discovered he's also an accuser of almighty God. Satan will do anything he can to drive a wedge between you and your loving Creator. He points a finger at God when tragedy—or even just circumstances you don't like—strikes. He suggests God doesn't care about your problems. He blames God for not healing your sick loved one.

All of these accusations come as subtle suggestions, whispers to your soul intended to make you bitter toward God because you feel disappointed, disillusioned, or deceived. Nothing is ever God's fault, but the devil can surely introduce doubt, ask a well-timed question, or arrange circumstantial evidence to set God up.

Don't fall for it. Satan is trying to get you to turn your back on the One who can help you through the disappointment, disillusionment, and deception. And if you are holding a grudge against God, He is ready to deliver you from the gall of bitterness. He's not mad at you, even though you've been mad at Him. Let's take a look at some examples in Scripture of how the devil accuses God.

> Now the serpent was more cunning than any beast of the field which the LORD God had made. And he said to the woman, "Has God indeed said, 'You shall not eat of every tree of the garden'?"
> —GENESIS 3:1, NKJV

This accusation against God, slight as it is, ultimately led to the fall of man. You know the story.

The woman said to the serpent, "We may eat the fruit of the trees of the garden; but of the fruit of the tree which is in the midst of the garden, God has said, 'You shall not eat it, nor shall you touch it, lest you die.'"

Then the serpent said to the woman, "You will not surely die. For God knows that in the day you eat of it your eyes will be opened, and you will be like God, knowing good and evil."

—GENESIS 3:2–5, NKJV

The devil accused God of lying to Adam. We know that "God is not a man, that He should lie" (Num. 23:19). More than that, the devil accused God of withholding something good to oppress His creation. When God arrived on the scene and asked Adam what he had done, Adam blamed Eve. Eve blamed the serpent. But it all started with the serpent accusing God. The rest is human history. Mankind has lived in corrupted, sinful flesh ever since because Eve believed a lie about God.

Ultimately you need to repent for buying into the devil's lies and accusations against God. But often that repentance won't come at a heart level until you've wrestled with God through the feelings of disappointment, disillusionment, and deception. So if you are mad at God, be honest with Him. It's not like He doesn't already know it. Give Him your anger, and He will turn that anger into peace and a greater revelation of His sovereignty if you will let Him. Amen.

USE *the*
ISAIAH 22:22 KEY

JESUS GAVE US the keys to the kingdom, and whatever we bind on earth shall be bound in heaven and whatever we loose on earth shall be loosed in heaven (Matt. 16:19). As spiritual warriors, many of us have become experts at binding and loosing.

But there's another key that believers can use to open doors that no one can shut and shut doors that no one can open. The Word of God reveals this prophetic key in both the Old and New Testaments. It's the key of David. Some call it the Isaiah 22:22 key, but you could also call it the Revelation 3:7 key because the prophetic scripture is mentioned in both books.

Isaiah 22:22 reads, "The key of the house of David I will lay on his shoulder. Then he shall open, and no one shall shut. And he shall shut, and no one shall open." The NLT translates it this way: "I will give him the key to the house of David—the highest position in the royal court. When he opens doors, no one will be able to close them; when he closes doors, no one will be able to open them."

Revelation 3:7 says, "He who is holy, He who is true, He who has the key of David, He who opens and no one shuts, and shuts and no one opens..." Of course, the "He" in these verses is Jesus. Jesus has the key and can open and shut as He wills. When Jesus opens the door, no man can shut it, and when Jesus shuts the door, no man can open it. Our job as prophetic people is to discern His will and kingdom purpose so we can exercise our authority in His name to open what He wants opened and shut what He wants shut.

Again, the key is discerning His will. Jesus has not called us to be reckless with the key of David, nor will the Isaiah 22:22 key work if we try to turn it in a direction opposite His will. But when we hear from the Lord, we can turn that key with confidence and decree and declare that doors will open or close. It's a powerful prophetic act that breaks down barriers.

The Isaiah 22:22 key also carries a governmental authority. Through our intercession and Spirit-inspired prophetic acts, we can impact our society. Jesus told us to occupy until He comes (Luke 19:13, KJV). The key of David—or the Isaiah 22:22 key—is not merely for unlocking doors in your life. It's for unlocking doors in your city. It's not just for locking the door on the enemy's plans for your family. It's for locking doors of access in your city. So discern His will and use the Isaiah 22:22 key to open and shut doors as the Lord directs.

Spiritual Warfare Tactic 63

AVOID
SELF-PITY

Self-pity attracts devils. Self-pity, by its very definition, is self-indulgence. When the enemy starts attacking you full throttle, meddling in your circumstances, and working overtime on your mind, there is a strong temptation to feel sorry for yourself.

This is the wrong response to spiritual warfare. No matter what kind of blow you take from the enemy, self-pity will hold you back from your mission to go up and recover all. Self-pity is one of the enemy's prime strategies for imprisoning your soul.

When self-pity manifests, you feel as if no one could possibly understand what you are going through. So you sit and lick your demon-inspired hurts and wounds and focus on self, self, self. You need to focus instead on Jesus, Jesus, Jesus. The people around you may not understand the pain you are going through, but Jesus understands. He was wounded doing the will of His Father. He was betrayed doing the work of God. He gets it. Hebrews 4:15–16 tells us:

> For we do not have a High Priest who cannot sympathize with our weaknesses, but One who was in every sense tempted like we are, yet without sin. Let us then come with confidence to the throne of grace, that we may obtain mercy and find grace to help in time of need.

You need to run to Jesus when the temptation to pity yourself arises. He doesn't feel sorry for you, but He does have compassion on you, and He will help you rise to fight another day.

Elijah fell into the self-pity trap. After he received a death threat from Jezebel, "he went a day's journey into the wilderness and came and sat down under a juniper tree and asked that he might die, saying, 'It is enough! Now, O Lord, take my life, for I am not better than my fathers'" (1 Kings 19:4). Elijah told the Lord, "I have been very zealous for the Lord, Lord of Hosts, for the children of Israel have forsaken Your covenant, thrown down Your altars, and killed Your prophets with the sword, and I alone am left, and they seek to take my life" (v. 10). And he said that to the Lord more than once.

Sounds sort of like Jonah sitting under the gourd (Jon. 4:6), doesn't it? Have you ever been in a place where you said, "God, just take me on to heaven now. I can't deal with this anymore"? I'll admit that I have. If God was listening (later I always hope He wasn't), He didn't even dignify my whining with an answer.

Elijah wanted to die right then and there, or so he said. He took his focus off God and put it on himself. He fell into the trap of self-pity. He felt lonely. If this happens to you, seek those of your own company. Don't let Jezebel isolate you from the brethren. You are not alone.

Recognize self-pity for what it is: a demonic assignment to get you focused on yourself instead of focusing on your deliverer. When you focus on who God is for you and in you, you can't possibly fall into the self-pity trap. Remember, "You will keep him in perfect peace, whose mind is stayed on You, because he trusts in You" (Isa. 26:3).

Spiritual Warfare Tactic 64

STOP WHINING
ABOUT *the* WARFARE

WHINING AND COMPLAINING will not stop the warfare and combat. In fact, whining, complaining, moaning, criticizing, griping, fretting, grumbling, lamenting, bellyaching, bewailing, fussing, grousing, sniveling, wailing, whimpering, and yammering will only magnify the warfare in your eyes. Say all that three times fast next time you feel like complaining.

Warriors are not wimps, and complainers are not conquerors. You are not a victim; you are a victorious overcomer. God intends you to win every battle and always leads you into triumph in Christ (2 Cor. 2:14). You enforce His victory in your life by faith and grace. Although whining about the warfare doesn't dull the sword of the Spirit, which is the Word of God (Eph. 6:17), it does dull your spirit to His leading.

In Philippians 2:14–15 Paul admonished us by the Spirit of God to "do all things without murmuring and disputing, that you may be blameless and harmless, sons of God, without fault, in the midst of a crooked and perverse generation, in which you shine as lights in the world." When you complain, you're acting like the world—and like the devil. You are demonstrating your discontent with God. You're actually complaining against God! Paul could have complained when he was beaten, shipwrecked, falsely accused, betrayed, and otherwise persecuted. But he learned the secret to being content in any situation: he discovered he could do anything with Christ's strength flowing through him (Phil. 4:11–13). When the enemy comes at you, don't complain; cry out to God for strength to endure the battle.

When you start whining and complaining, you've stopped walking in the Spirit and stepped into the flesh. Maintaining the fruit of the Spirit in your life is a defense against the enemy's plot to influence your flesh. Paul reveals in Galatians 5:22–25:

> But the fruit of the Spirit is love, joy, peace, patience, gentleness, goodness, faith, meekness, and self-control; against such there is no law. Those who are Christ's have crucified the flesh with its passions and lusts. If we live in the Spirit, let us also walk in the Spirit.

By contrast, Paul revealed the works of the flesh and the consequences of consistently walking in them: "adultery, sexual immorality, impurity, lewdness, idolatry, sorcery, hatred, strife, jealousy, rage, selfishness, dissensions, heresies, envy, murders, drunkenness, carousing, and the like. I warn you, as I previously warned you, that those who do such things shall not inherit the kingdom of God" (Gal. 5:19–21).

Although he doesn't specifically mention complaining, he does say, "and the like." We know that murmuring displeases God and have seen this practice impact inheritances in Scripture. Specifically, in reference to the Israelites in the wilderness who did not enter into the Promised Land because of their evil report, Paul writes, "Neither murmur, as some of them also murmured and were destroyed by the destroyer" (1 Cor. 10:10).

The Greek word for murmur is *goggyzō*, and its definition may surprise you. It not only means "to murmur, mutter, grumble, say anything against in a low tone," but it also means "of those who discontentedly complain."[1] Sometimes we don't complain to others openly, but we complain to God under our breath or in a "low tone." We express our discontent in the midst of warfare, and in doing so, we're swinging a carnal sword against ourselves instead of swinging the sword of the Spirit that would ultimately make us content in victory over our adversary.

REJOICE *in* *the* LORD

Rejoice in the Lord always. Again I will say, rejoice!" (Phil. 4:4). Those were the Spirit-inspired words of Paul the apostle. Historians tell us Paul penned his letter to the Philippian church from prison. Although which prison is still debated, does it really matter? He was in bondage to the world system, under attack by men influenced by the principalities and powers he described so aptly in Ephesians 6:12.

Of Paul's setting, Rick Renner said in a sermon that an expert in early church history told him, "At the time that the apostle Paul was held in this prison, it was the central holding tank for the sewage system of the city of Rome. Most men who were held in this place were killed by the smell. The toxins in this place were so terrible that just breathing them would asphyxiate you to death. That's what this was when the apostle Paul was here. And on certain days, if the wind is just right and if the heat is just right, like today, you can still smell the sewage of 2,000 years ago. That is the smell that you are smelling; this is sewage from 2,000 years ago."[1]

If Paul could rejoice in this type of natural and spiritual warfare, why can't we? The truth is, we can. We can choose to rejoice. Nobody can stop us from rejoicing in the Lord in our hearts. And we should make this choice quickly because the joy of the Lord is our strength (Neh. 8:10).

Take a page out of David's playbook: "But may all those who seek refuge in You rejoice; may they ever shout for joy, because You defend them; may those who love Your name be joyful in You" (Ps. 5:11). And again, "This is the day that the LORD has made; we will rejoice and be glad in it" (Ps. 118:24). And again, "Bless the LORD, O my soul, and all that is within me, bless His holy name. Bless the LORD, O my soul, and forget not all His benefits, who forgives all your iniquities, who heals all your diseases, who redeems your life from the pit, who crowns you with lovingkindness and tender mercies, who satisfies your mouth with good things, so that your youth is renewed like the eagle's" (Ps. 103:1–5).

Rejoicing in the Lord is not a suggestion. It's a command—a truth that will set you free. First Thessalonians 5:16 sums it up in two words: "Rejoice always."

If you can't find anything else to rejoice about, rejoice in the joy of your salvation. Remember the joy—the burden that came off your back—when you accepted Jesus. It's likely you were miserable—or at least discontent and desperate for change—at the moment you invited Jesus into your heart as Lord and Savior. You can pray this prayer:

> Restore to me the joy of Your salvation, and uphold me with Your willing spirit. Then I will teach transgressors Your ways, and sinners will return to You (Ps. 51:12–13). Give me the grace to rejoice in You with my whole heart. Help me to bless Your name day and night, night and day, because You are faithful. I put my trust in You and rejoice in the outcome.

Spiritual Warfare Tactic 66

PUSH BACK
the DARKNESS

In Ephesians 6:12 Paul speaks of the "rulers of the darkness of this world." There are demon powers that rule in darkness. One translation says, "powers of this dark world" (NIV). Another says, "mighty powers in this dark world" (NLT). Still others say, "the cosmic powers over this present darkness" (ESV), "the world forces of this darkness" (NASB), and "powers that govern this world of darkness" (NASB 1977).

The word *rulers* in Paul's phrase *rulers of the darkness of this world* comes from the Greek word *kosmokratōr*. It means "lord of the world, prince of this age."[1] But what is this darkness they rule over? *Darkness* in this verse comes from the Greek word *skotos*. It can mean "darkness; of night darkness." But in this context it means "of ignorance respecting divine things and human duties, and the accompanying ungodliness and immorality, together with their consequent misery in hell." It also means, "persons in whom darkness becomes visible and holds sway."[2]

According to *The Pulpit Commentary*, "'This darkness' expressively denotes the element and the results of their rule. Observe contrast with Christ's servants, who are children of light, equivalent to order, knowledge, purity, joy, peace, etc.; while the element of the devil and his servants is darkness, equivalent to confusion, ignorance, crime, terror, strife, and all misery."[3]

Where you find confusion, ignorance, crime, terror, strife, and all misery, you find rulers of the darkness of this world at work. Thanks be to God, we were translated out of the kingdom of darkness and into the kingdom of His dear Son (Col. 1:13) and into His marvelous light (1 Pet. 2:9). We are citizens of the kingdom of light. We are children of light (1 Thess. 5:5). We are the light of the world in Christ (Matt. 5:14). When we follow Jesus, we will not walk in darkness; rather we will have the light of life (John 8:12).

There is no darkness in God (1 John 1:5), and His Word is a lamp unto our feet and a light unto our path (Ps. 119:105). Light always overcomes darkness—and it takes only a small amount of light to overpower pitch-black darkness.

We are called to expose the unfruitful works of darkness (Eph. 5:11) rather than fellowshipping with darkness (2 Cor. 6:14). As children of the light operating in the power of God, we have authority to push back darkness. How do you do this? When Jesus walked the earth, His overarching mission was to destroy the works of the devil as He went about doing good (Acts 10:38). He worked to push back the devil's dark deeds with the power of forgiveness, healing, and deliverance and otherwise contended against Satan's kingdom.

You can decree and declare, "I push back darkness, in the name of Jesus." But following it up by doing good is a keen strategy for overcoming evil. The Bible says, after all, that we overcome evil with good (Rom. 12:21). When we allow Jesus to send us on missions to help and heal, we are putting works with our faith to push back darkness.

WITHSTAND WEARINESS

WEARINESS IS A weapon of the enemy's warfare, and it is especially effective in persuading even the fiercest spiritual warriors to quit and give up. *Weary* means "exhausted in strength, endurance, vigor, or freshness."[1] When you are exhausted, you are completely worn out, consumed, and drained. You are in a weakened condition. Weariness puts you right where the devil wants you: mentally frazzled, bleary-eyed, and beat down spiritually and physically.

Daniel 7:25 lays out this demonic strategy with crystal clarity: "He shall speak words against the Most High and shall wear out the saints of the Most High." The NASB says "wear down the saints." The NET Bible says "harass." The NIV says "oppress." The Jubilee Bible 2000 says "break down." The Douay-Rheims Bible says "crush." That about sums it up. It all spells utter exhaustion.

How does the enemy wear you out, wear you down, harass you, oppress you, break you down, and crush you to the point of exhaustion? Many times it is through his words that defy God's promises in your life. He wears you down through vain imaginations that exalt themselves against God's Word—that is, vain imaginations you don't capture and cast down (2 Cor. 10:5).

Yet in Galatians 6 we find the Holy Spirit admonishing us not to allow weariness to set in: "And let us not grow weary in doing good, for in due season we shall reap, if we do not give up" (v. 9). We must not allow ourselves to grow weary in fighting the good fight of faith (1 Tim. 6:12).

Galatians 6:9 implies that this assignment against the enemy works over time. Nothing grows overnight, not children, not the fruit of the Spirit, not our knowledge of the Bible. Growth implies seedtime and harvesttime. You will see a harvest of victory if you don't give up.

Clearly, there's a tension between Daniel 7:25 and Galatians 6:9. God spells out the enemy's strategy with precision to give us a heads up. The Lord is saying essentially, "The devil is going to come to wear you out with fierce lies about you and about My Word. He's going to try as hard as he can to completely drain you of strength."

Make no mistake, God knows the battle against our minds will be fierce. Nevertheless, He tells us straight out not to grow weary. If He tells us not to grow weary, then it's possible not to grow weary. He would not give us a battle instruction that we could not carry out.

At the first sign of weariness, you have to use common sense and Bible sense. From a natural perspective, when we are truly tired or hungry, it can be more difficult to see things from God's perspective. If we're not getting quality sleep, quality food, and quality fellowship to strengthen our bodies and souls, we are more susceptible to weariness. Don't make decisions in this state.

From a spiritual perspective we need to follow the advice of Jesus Himself when He walked the earth: "Take My yoke upon you and learn of Me, for I am gentle (meek) and humble (lowly) in heart, and you will find rest (relief and ease and refreshment and recreation and blessed quiet) for your souls. For My yoke is wholesome (useful, good—not harsh, hard, sharp, or pressing, but comfortable, gracious, and pleasant), and My burden is light and easy to be borne" (Matt. 11:29–30, AMPC).

STAY SPIRITUALLY ALERT

Y OU'VE HEARD IT said that the enemy doesn't fight fair. Well, that's a spiritual warfare understatement if I've ever heard one. The devil is a dirty fighter, and he's just as subtle as he is dirty. He never sleeps or slumbers, but he works to put us to sleep through apathy, complacency, and waves of weariness.

We know there is an enemy lurking around like a roaring lion seeking to devour us. Peter is extremely clear about this spiritual reality: "Be well balanced (temperate, sober of mind), be vigilant and cautious at all times; for that enemy of yours, the devil, roams around like a lion roaring [in fierce hunger], seeking someone to seize upon and devour" (1 Pet. 5:8, AMPC).

If this was a physical, flesh-and-blood enemy roaming around trying to kill us, steal from us, or destroy what belongs to us, then we would be on red alert at all times much as the protagonists in action and adventure movies are. What we often fail to understand is the unseen world is more real than what we can see with our eyes. The seen world will fade away. The unseen world is eternal—and there are devils on the loose!

Sadly many Christians are not spiritually alert and they're getting devoured. They're miserable. They're discouraged. They're upset. They're in strife. The enemy is devouring their money, devouring their time, devouring their children, devouring their health—killing, stealing, and destroying anything he can. We have to stay spiritually alert.

Many scriptures admonish us along these lines. We need to meditate on these verses until the need to wake up and stay awake renews our minds to the reality of the war. We don't have to be afraid. We just have to be alert.

> But know this, that if the owner of the house had known what hour the thief would come, he would have watched and not have let his house be broken into.
>
> —MATTHEW 24:43

> What I say to you I say to all: Watch!
>
> —MARK 13:37

> Watch and pray, lest you enter into temptation. The spirit indeed is willing, but the flesh is weak.
>
> —MARK 14:38

> Therefore watch always and pray.
>
> —LUKE 21:36

> Pray in the Spirit always with all kinds of prayer and supplication. To that end be alert with all perseverance and supplication for all the saints.
>
> —EPHESIANS 6:18

Jesus teaches in the parable of the tares that the enemy sows tares—what we would call weeds in today's world—while the farmer is asleep. We must stay spiritually alert to our thought life as the enemy works to sow demonic seeds in our minds.

We must not remove our belt of truth and embrace lies. We must not set down the sword of the Spirit and pick up fleshly habits. We must not take off the breastplate of righteousness, compromising who we are in Christ to avoid conflict in the workplace or in the church or even in the pulpit. We must not trade in our shoes of peace for chaos. We must stay awake to the spiritual war so we can resist the enemy before he sows his wicked seeds.

OBLITERATE
FEAR

FEAR HAS NO right to enter your life. Fear is part of the curse of the law as found in Deuteronomy 28:66: "Your life shall hang in doubt before you. You will be in dread day and night and will have no assurance of your life." The good news is Jesus "redeemed us from the curse of the law by being made a curse for us" (Gal. 3:13).

Faith without action is dead. Fear without action lives. So you have to take action against it! Perhaps you are scared of spiritual warfare because you skinned your knee, lost a skirmish, or sustained friendly fire in a battle. Maybe you fear stepping out into something new because you might get hit upside the head with the devil's demonic baseball bat.

Fear flings wide the door of your heart to spiritual attack. Whatever is not of faith is sin (Rom. 14:23), and fear is not of faith. Fear is diametrically opposed to faith. You can't walk by faith and walk by fear at the same time. You can't enter the battlefield with fear because it's akin to having a crack in your shield of faith.

Take a page from Gideon's story in the Bible. The Lord told Gideon, "'So now, call out so the people can hear, "Whoever is afraid or anxious may turn back and leave Mount Gilead."' So twenty-two thousand from among the people turned back, and ten thousand were left" (Judg. 7:3). Fear will always attack you in the face of war.

Likewise, we know that the Israelite army under King Saul's command allowed fear to delay a great victory God ordained for them in the Valley at Sokoh. Goliath, a champion from the enemy Philistine army, was provoking Israel to war. He charged

Israel with sending out one man to fight him in the valley. First Samuel 17:11 reveals the condition of their hearts: "When Saul and all Israel heard these words of the Philistine, they were filled with terror and were greatly afraid."

You need to be like David and run to the battle line despite the enemy's threats, having God-like faith that defies every threat.

If you don't identify and face your fear, you will not live God's best life for you. By contrast, when you identify your fear, you can face it with the sword of the Spirit in your mouth, defeat it, and gain the spoils of war. Victory starts with getting fear out of your mind and out of your mouth. Stop confessing the fearful thoughts the devil whispers to your soul, and you won't fuel the fear.

You have to give fear permission to wreak havoc on your life. It's time to face your fears. I am believing the Holy Spirit will reveal to you any hidden fears plaguing your life so you can confront and conquer them and live the abundant life Jesus died to give you. And if you have a fear of confrontation, it's time to overcome that also.

Obliterate fear. You don't need to fear the devil. The devil needs to fear you. You need to fear the Lord.

CLOSE *the* DOOR
on STRIFE

STRIFE SPREADS LIKE wildfire. And it's not always as obvious as bickering on the worship team, screaming in workplace staff meetings, or behind-the-door browbeating on the home front.

Strife, which *Merriam-Webster* defines as "bitter sometimes violent conflict or dissension; an act of contention; exertion or contention for superiority,"[1] opens the door wide to the enemy. If you see it, you need to root it out and repent for your part immediately.

So, what does strife look like and what causes it? Where you see power struggles and exertion of superiority, you can't automatically blame Jezebel. Strife is the likely motivator. When you see arguing or contending over anything, it's not always rebellion. Strife is typically lurking.

Strife is an abomination to God (Prov. 6:16–19). Strife affects the anointing and the flow of the Holy Ghost (Ps. 133:1–3). Strife grieves the Holy Spirit (Eph. 4:29–32). Strife destroys relationships (Prov. 17:9). Strife is rooted in anger (Prov. 29:22), hatred (Prov. 10:12), pride (Prov. 13:10), and a quarrelsome, self-seeking spirit (Luke 22:24–27; Gal. 5:14–17). James put it this way:

> Where do wars and fights come from among you? Do they not come from your desires for pleasure that war in your members? You lust and do not have. You murder and covet and cannot obtain. You fight and war. Yet you do not have because you do not ask. You ask and do not receive, because you ask amiss, that you may spend it on your pleasures.
>
> —JAMES 4:1–3, NKJV

It was James who also said this:

> But if ye have bitter envying and strife in your hearts, glory
> not, and lie not against the truth. This wisdom descendeth
> not from above, but is earthly, sensual, devilish. For where
> envying and strife is, there is confusion and every evil work.
> —JAMES 3:14–16, KJV

Let me repeat what James wrote so you don't miss it: "where
envying and strife is, there is confusion and every evil work." Strife
opens the door to principalities, powers, rulers of the darkness of
this age, and spiritual hosts of wickedness in the heavenly places.
Strife opens the door to spiritual warfare.

The Bible also offers strong warnings against strife. Paul warns,
"But if you bite and devour one another [in partisan strife], be
careful that you [and your whole fellowship] are not consumed by
one another" (Gal. 5:15, AMPC). When there was strife between the
herdsmen of Abraham and Lot, the elder was wise enough to separate himself from it.

If you find yourself under attack, look for strife in your life. It
may be in your heart or it may be in the heart of another against
you because of envy. Get on your face and worship God. Repent
of anything He shows you that is not right in your own heart.
Then ask Him what the source of the warfare is. Nothing kills the
anointing faster than strife. Don't lie against the truth. If strife is
the root of your spiritual warfare, repent so you can see clearly to
battle your other spiritual enemies.

MAKE *a*
BATTLE PLAN

Before you head into battle, you need to take some time to make a battle plan. A battle plan is the strategy you will use to engage the enemy. It's a plan for dealing a death blow to your spiritual opposition. Military generals do not step foot on the battlefield without a battle plan—and neither should you. Jesus gave us insight in Luke 14:31–32 (AMPC):

> Or what king, going out to engage in conflict with another king, will not first sit down and consider and take counsel whether he is able with ten thousand [men] to meet him who comes against him with twenty thousand? And if he cannot [do so], when the other king is still a great way off, he sends an envoy and asks the terms of peace.

Drafting your battle plan starts with considering and taking counsel with God. If God is not leading you into battle, then don't go. When you consider and take counsel with God, He will give you the battle plan.

Many times David inquired of the Lord, "Shall I go up?" (e.g., 2 Sam. 5:19). God always answered him, sometimes with greater detail than others. Other times David was warned about an enemy and retreated to a stronghold.

Once you have looked at the question of whether or not to fight, you need to take it a step further and find out how to fight. There is a strong example of how the Lord can give a detailed battle plan in 2 Samuel 5:22–25:

Once again, the Philistines went up and spread out in the Valley of Rephaim. When David inquired of the LORD, He said, "You shall not go up. Circle around behind them and come against them opposite the trees. When you hear the sound of marching in the tops of the trees, pay attention, because at that point the LORD is going before you to defeat the army of the Philistines." So David did just as the LORD commanded, and he defeated the Philistines from Geba as far as Gezer.

Joshua also had a battle plan to enter into the Promised Land. In Joshua 6 the battle plan included marching around the city once a day for six days, then seven times on the seventh day with priests blowing the trumpet. When the ram's horn blew, the people shouted and walls of Jericho fell down. God's battle plan for Gideon was to weed out thousands of men and leave the mighty man of valor with just three hundred. (See Judges 7.) God's battle plan for Jehoshaphat was to praise his way. He didn't even have to fight the battle. (See 2 Chronicles 20.)

Be careful not to use the same battle plan for every spiritual skirmish. Ask the Lord what the battle plan is, what weapons of warfare to use, when the right time is to strike, who to enlist as intercessors to stand with you, what to bind, what to loose, what key to use, and what prayers to pray. Don't step onto the battlefield until you get at least step one of the plan.

ASK *the* LORD *to* OPEN YOUR EYES *to the* SPIRIT REALM

ITʼS BEEN SAID we donʼt know what we donʼt know, but itʼs just as true that we canʼt see what we canʼt see. Sometimes the enemy has so clouded our vision that we need God to break in with light—to open our eyes wide so we can see the supernatural events unfolding behind the natural scenes.

When God opens our eyes, it may be in the form of a prophetic dream, a vision, a trance, or even what feels like a real-life experience in heaven or hell. Although we should not seek supernatural experiences for the sake of seeking supernatural experiences, we should seek God and trust that He will give us what we need. Thereʼs nothing wrong with crying out to God to open your eyes when you sense that you arenʼt seeing what He really wants you to see.

In Elishaʼs day the king of Syria was warring against Israel. The prophet Elisha gave the Israelites a marked advantage—he was able to hear the words Syriaʼs king spoke in his bedroom, and he relayed them to the king of Israel (2 Kings 6:12). The Syrian king wanted Elisha stopped and sent out horses, chariots, and a great army to fetch him. When he saw the Syrian army surrounding the city, Elishaʼs servant got scared.

> And his servant said to him, "Alas, my master! What will we do?"
>
> And he said, "Do not be afraid, for there are more with us than with them." Then Elisha prayed, "LORD, open his eyes and let him see." So the LORD opened the eyes of

the young man, and he saw that the mountain was full of horses and chariots of fire surrounding Elisha.

—2 Kings 6:15–17

What confidence Elisha's servant must have gained, not just in that moment but throughout his walk with the Lord. And that brings me to Paul's prayer for the church at Ephesus, which is something I would suggest praying over yourself daily. In this prayer Paul asks the Lord to open the believers' eyes for a specific purpose—a purpose that is sure to spark faith in soul and spirit:

> Therefore I also, after hearing of your faith in the Lord Jesus and your love toward all the saints, do not cease giving thanks for you, mentioning you in my prayers, so that the God of our Lord Jesus Christ, the Father of glory, may give you the Spirit of wisdom and revelation in the knowledge of Him, that the eyes of your understanding may be enlightened, that you may know what is the hope of His calling and what are the riches of the glory of His inheritance among the saints, and what is the surpassing greatness of His power toward us who believe, according to the working of His mighty power.
>
> —Ephesians 1:15–19

We all have blind spots, whether it's personally or with spiritual warfare. So cry out to God, ask Him to flood your heart with light, open your eyes, and show you what He wants you to see.

MAKE *a* DECISION
NOT *to* GIVE UP

IF YOU'RE LIKE me, there are times when you feel like God just isn't listening. Mean voices are rising with guilt and condemnation or angry slander. You feel like you've prayed your guts out. You're battling fear. You just want to fly away, to escape the warfare. You want to run off to a cabin in the woods. You need a break from the battle, and you need it now. You've tried everything and nothing changes. You are on the verge of giving up.

So, what do you do when you feel like giving up? Do you go on a sleep marathon, hoping to escape the harsh reality? Do you veg out in front of the television with a bag of potato chips and a pint of ice cream (and put on a few pounds), watching anything that will keep your mind off the pain? Do you call your friends to rehearse and rehash the drama, hoping they will have a **prophetic word**? Do you wallow in self-pity? Do you drown your pillow with tears (Ps. 6:6)? I've done all those things, but none of it helps.

So, what *should* you do when you feel like giving up? Keep going. You have to determine in your heart long before the battle begins raging that you will not give up under any circumstance. The temptation to give up will work to absolutely overwhelm you if you don't set your mind to persevere before the enemy engages you in sudden warfare.

I know all too well what it feels like to want to give up. I know all too well the temptations to revert to the world's comfort in the midst of the warfare. I know all too well the emotions that come with a raging storm against your family. But quitting is simply not an option. If you lay your weapons down, the devil won't just forfeit his position and pursue someone else. If you lay your weapons down, you just become an easier target for the enemy. The devil will keep attacking until he has robbed you of your faith to believe in the goodness of God.

When you feel like giving up, you can take your complaints to God. He can certainly handle it. Like David, you can take your deep sighs to God dusk, dawn, and noon. But ultimately you have to come to the conclusion that God does hear you (Ps. 116:1), that He is working on the situation (Rom. 8:28), and that His grace is sufficient for you (2 Cor. 12:9). You have to conclude God is trustworthy (Ps. 9:10). And you have to keep on the whole armor of God so you are able to withstand the attacks of the enemy against your mind and, having done all, stand (Eph. 6:13). Refuse to not stand.

Pile your troubles on God's shoulders. If He carried David's load and helped David out—and He did—then He won't fail you. As trite as it sounds, set your heart to trust in God, and you will not be disappointed (Rom. 10:11). Don't give up. If you don't quit, you will win.

FAST WITH FEAR
and TREMBLING

WHEN LED BY the Spirit, fasting can be a strategic warfare tactic. Notice I said, "When led by the Spirit." If you walk with the Spirit, He will tell you when to fast as a warfare strategy. When your fasting is Spirit-led, there will be a grace on you to abstain from food or anything else He may instruct you to fast from, such as television, sports, or some other activity that's distracting you from His heart.

When there's an intense war ahead, many times the Spirit of God will indeed lead you to fast weeks or days ahead of time to crucify your flesh. This is His kindness toward you, a way of preparing you to strengthen your resolve so you will avoid the temptation to "flesh out" when the demonic pressure comes.

It's important to crucify your flesh because that carnal nature wars against His will. Specifically, Galatians 5:17 says the flesh wars against the Spirit and the Spirit wars against the flesh. When you are in a heated battle, you don't want your flesh agreeing with the devil against God. Fasting kills carnal tendencies.

There are many significant spiritual benefits to fasting before, during, and after spiritual warfare. When you fast—and, to be clear, Jesus said, "When you fast" (Matt. 6:16), not "If you fast"— you humble your soul (Ps. 69:10). You need humility in the battle because humility attracts God's grace. God's grace is His power, His favor, and His ability to do what you cannot do in your own strength.

Fasting makes you more sensitive to the Spirit, and you need to remain more sensitive to the Spirit in times of warfare. You need to hear that still, small voice. You need His battle plan, His strategies, His tactics. Fasting helps you cultivate an intimacy with Jesus that will guard you against offense against Him during the battle. (See Mark 2:20.)

Sometimes you have to fast to break a yoke, especially if your fleshly habits allowed the enemy entrance. Repent, fast, and pray. Isaiah 58:6 tells us, "Is not this the fast that I have chosen: to loose the bonds of wickedness, to undo the heavy burdens, and to let the oppressed go free, and break every yoke?" And remember when the disciples could not cast the demon out of the boy with the unclean spirit? After Jesus cast the demon out, when the disciples asked Him about it privately, He answered plainly: "This kind cannot come out except by prayer and fasting" (Mark 9:29).

Remember, fasting doesn't change God, but it does change you. You don't fast to cajole God into doing something. God wants to give you overwhelming victory against every enemy. But your soul wants you to move in the realm of overwhelm and your flesh wants to overpower you with anti-God temptations that keep you trapped in demonic cycles.

REJECT PRESUMPTION *and* ASSUMPTION *in the* BATTLE

P RESUMPTION AND ASSUMPTION are dangerous in the spiritual warfare realm. David prayed to the Lord to keep him away from "presumptuous sin" (Ps. 19:13). We can walk in presumption while thinking we're walking in prudence because of past spiritual warfare teaching that was off the mark.

What does it mean to presume? And what exactly is presumption? *Merriam-Webster* defines *presume* as "to form an opinion from little or no evidence" and "to take as true or as fact without actual proof."[1] *Presumptuous* is defined as "overstepping due bounds; taking liberties."[2] Those definitions outline some critical spiritual warfare dos and don'ts. There is no room for personal opinion in the realm of discernment. Our discernment must come from the Holy Spirit, not our souls.

Assume means "to take to or upon oneself; to pretend to have or be; to take as granted or true."[3] We cannot assume warfare that is not ours. We cannot fake our way through battles. We cannot take for granted that we are experts against any given spirit.

Doubtless, God hates presumption—and He has good reason. There are several variations of the word *presume* in the Bible. Typically the word portrays insolence (being "insultingly contemptuous in speech or conduct"[4]), pride, arrogance, or audacity ("bold or arrogant disregard for normal restraints"[5]).[6] Considering that the Lord includes a proud look and a false witness among the seven abominations, presumption is not something to be taken lightly.

In fact, while the King James Version of the Bible only mentions the words *presume*, *presumed*, *presumptuous*, and *presumptuously* eleven times, it almost always leads to death. Indeed, there are few things worse than a presumptuous prophet. Deuteronomy 18:20 declares, "But the prophet, which shall presume to speak a word in my name, which I have not commanded him to speak, or that shall speak in the name of other gods, even that prophet shall die" (KJV).

Mercy! Of course, we are living in a time of grace and even the most presumptuous spiritual warriors probably won't be struck dead for this sin. But presumption can still be dangerous in the spirit realm, especially if we wage war against principalities on our own. Jude 9 tells us, "But even the archangel Michael, when he disputed with the devil over the body of Moses, did not presume to bring a slanderous judgment against him, but said, 'The Lord rebuke you!'" (BSB).

There are needless casualties of war in the spirit realm because people overstepped due bounds of their authority, their assignment, their revelation, or even Scripture. We must not take liberties in the spirit realm that Christ has not given us. We must not wage war based on someone else's revelation, but from the revelation we receive from the Lord. We must avoid presumption and assumption and wait upon the Lord for discernment.

Spiritual Warfare Tactic 76

REMIND GOD
of HIS PROMISES

When you are standing on the promises of God, whether from His Word or a prophetic promise, the enemy always comes with strategies designed to steal the promise from your heart. Remember, the devil is not really coming for you; he's coming for the word that was planted in your heart. He's coming for the harvest that seed in word form will produce if you continue watering it with your faith. He's coming to defy the will of the Lord in your life.

In that moment you must decide if you will give up or if you will go back to the author, remind Him of what He said, and plead with Him to bring it to pass. Isaiah 43:26 says, "Put Me in remembrance; let us plead together; state your cause, that you may be justified."

Jacob got a prophetic word from God while he was fleeing his angry brother, Esau, whom he cheated out of his birthright. The prophecy was exceedingly abundantly above all he could ask or think:

> I am the Lord God of Abraham your father and the God of Isaac; the land on which you lie I will give to you and your descendants. Also your descendants shall be as the dust of the earth; you shall spread abroad to the west and the east, to the north and the south; and in you and in your seed all the families of the earth shall be blessed. Behold, I am with you and will keep you wherever you go, and will bring you back to this land; for I will not leave you until I have done what I have spoken to you.
>
> —Genesis 28:13–15, nkjv

Jacob believed the prophetic word. Despite being cheated by his uncle Laban for more than a decade, he prospered wildly. When he got fed up with Laban's dishonesty, he decided to return to his country. Along the way he heard Esau was coming out to meet him and fear struck his heart.

Jacob did what you need to do when it looks as if your prophetic word can't possibly come to pass, when it looks as if the devil is devouring your prophetic dreams. When the enemy comes in with fear that what God said will never happen, you need to take the prophetic word back to its author in prayer.

> Then Jacob said, "O God of my father Abraham and God of my father Isaac, the LORD who said to me, 'Return to your country and to your family, and I will deal well with you': I am not worthy of the least of all the mercies and of all the truth which You have shown Your servant; for I crossed over this Jordan with my staff, and now I have become two companies. Deliver me, I pray, from the hand of my brother, from the hand of Esau; for I fear him, lest he come and attack me and the mother with the children. For You said, 'I will surely treat you well, and make your descendants as the sand of the sea, which cannot be numbered for multitude.'"
>
> —GENESIS 32:9–12, NKJV

When you are facing warfare over the prophetic word God spoke to your heart, remind God of His prophetic word. Wrestle with God in prayer until you have the faith to get up and run toward His perfect will despite what things look like.

BE CONFIDENT GOD
IS *on* YOUR SIDE

I'M CONVINCED ONE of David's strongest advantages in battle was not merely the fact that God was on his side—but his deep and unshakable understanding that God was on his side. David was a fierce warrior. He pursued the enemies of Israel relentlessly, but he was also pursued relentlessly by his enemies.

David's revelation that God was on his side is evidenced in psalms like this one: "Do not deliver me to the will of my enemies; for false witnesses have risen against me, and they breathe out violence. I believe I will see the goodness of the LORD in the land of the living" (Ps. 27:12–13).

In many psalms David pours out his fear, sorrow, and frustration in the midst of the warfare. I'm grateful these episodes are recorded, demonstrating what faith under pressure looks like. David always ended his psalms with a demonstration of reliance on God.

Today we sing songs about how God is with us and how nothing can stop us, but many times in the hottest moments of a heated battle we find ourselves asking God where He is. We sometimes wonder if He is really on our side.

David did that too. In Psalm 22:1–2 he bemoaned, "My God, my God, why have You forsaken me? Why are You so far from delivering me, and from my roaring words of distress? O my God, I cry in the daytime, but You do not answer; and at night, but I have no rest." But he didn't stay there. He concluded God was with Him and praised Him.

Sometimes we can't hear God or see Him moving in a situation.

But we need to remind ourselves that although we can't see Him, touch Him, or hear Him, He is still on our side. Inspired by the Holy Spirit, Paul the apostle laid out one of the most convincing faith-building passages that God is on our side in Romans 8:31–39. We must meditate on this passage until we are utterly convinced He is fighting for us.

> If God is for us, who can be against us? He who did not spare His own Son, but delivered Him up for us all, how shall He not with Him also freely give us all things? Who shall bring a charge against God's elect? It is God who justifies. Who is he who condemns? It is Christ who died, yes, who is risen, who is also at the right hand of God, who also intercedes for us. Who shall separate us from the love of Christ? Shall tribulation, or distress, or persecution, or famine, or nakedness, or peril, or sword? As it is written: "For Your sake we are killed all day long; we are counted as sheep for the slaughter." No, in all these things we are more than conquerors through Him who loved us. For I am persuaded that neither death nor life, neither angels nor principalities nor powers, neither things present nor things to come, neither height nor depth, nor any other created thing, shall be able to separate us from the love of God, which is in Christ Jesus our Lord.

Amen!

Spiritual Warfare Tactic 78

WAR FROM *a*
POSITION *of* VICTORY

WHEN YOU WAR from a position or a mind-set of defeat, it's difficult to muster the faith you need to execute Christ's victory over the enemy of your soul. Warring from a position or a mind-set of victory will bring a swifter end to the battle most of the time.

Ephesians 1:19–23 (AMPC) makes your position crystal clear. If this truth isn't in you, your journey to entering the battlefield with your mind set on collecting the spoils of war starts here:

> And [so that you can know and understand] what is the immeasurable and unlimited and surpassing greatness of His power in and for us who believe, as demonstrated in the working of His mighty strength, which He exerted in Christ when He raised Him from the dead and seated Him at His [own] right hand in the heavenly [places], far above all rule and authority and power and dominion and every name that is named [above every title that can be conferred], not only in this age and in this world, but also in the age and the world which are to come. And He has put all things under His feet and has appointed Him the universal and supreme Head of the church [a headship exercised throughout the church], which is His body, the fullness of Him Who fills all in all [for in that body lives the full measure of Him Who makes everything complete, and Who fills everything everywhere with Himself].

If all things are under Christ's feet and you are one with Christ—and you are—then all things, including the devil, are under your feet also. What's more, Ephesians 2:6 (AMPC) emphasizes your position in Christ: "And He raised us up together with Him and made us sit down together [giving us joint seating with Him] in the heavenly sphere [by virtue of our being] in Christ Jesus (the Messiah, the Anointed One)."

Remember, Jesus "disarmed the principalities and powers that were ranged against us and made a bold display and public example of them, in triumphing over them in Him and in it [the cross]" (Col. 2:15, AMPC). That doesn't mean you don't have to fight. It just means you are warring from a position of victory. You are merely enforcing Christ's victory in the earth.

Put another way, you are not an underdog in the good fight of faith. The enemy knows he is defeated. All he has in his arsenal are lies that work to convince you that he has the advantage. Jesus has decreed and declared your victory. He paid the price for your breakthrough. There is no defeat in Jesus—ever. He's never lost a battle.

When Goliath challenged the army of Israel, the soldiers were scared witless of the Philistine champion. But David was a covenant man, and he understood that victory belonged to him in God. As believers we war from a position of victory, knowing that God always leads us in triumph in Christ (2 Cor. 2:14). "We are more than conquerors through Him who loved us" (Rom. 8:37). And, again, "If God is for us, who can be against us?" (v. 31).

BREAK ANY *and* ALL VOWS WITH *the* ENEMY

BEFORE YOU HEAD into battle, or if the Lord gives you a revelation you may have to call time-out and deal with this issue in the battle, be sure to break any agreement you have with the enemy.

Listen to your words. Catch your thoughts. How are you spending your time? Are you spending your time in a way that is glorifying the enemy? What kind of entertainment are you watching? What kind of music are you listening to? These things matter.

Beyond what you think, see, and hear in the world around you, though, there's another issue that many don't consider in the realm of victorious spiritual warfare: inner vows and resignations. God takes vows really seriously. Just how seriously? Consider these scriptures:

Numbers 30:2 says, "If a man vows a vow to the LORD or swears an oath to bind himself with a bond, he will not break his word. He will do according to all that proceeds out of his mouth." Deuteronomy 23:21 tells us: "When you make a vow to the LORD your God, you must not be slow to pay it, for the LORD your God will surely require it of you, and it would be a sin to you." And Ecclesiastes 5:4 says, "When you make a vow to God, do not delay in fulfilling it because He has no pleasure in fools. Fulfill what you have vowed."

The enemy also takes vows seriously. Jesus actually warns us not to make them at all: "But I say to you, do not swear at all: neither by heaven, for it is God's throne; nor by the earth, for it is His footstool; nor by Jerusalem, for it is the city of the great King. Nor shall you swear by your head, because you cannot make one hair white or black. But let your 'Yes' mean 'Yes,' and 'No' mean 'No.' For whatever is more than these comes from the evil one" (Matt. 5:34–37).

We often make vows as children or when some great harm comes to us. We may forget all about it, but the vow is still intact as the reality is that the power of death and life are in the tongue (Prov. 18:21).

Vows often include always/never statements. Here are some examples: I will never love again. I will never let anyone control me. I will never marry again. I will never let anyone know I am hurt. I will never be like my mother. I will always be poor. I will always struggle with relationships. Along the same lines as inner vows are death wishes, wishing you were dead or could go to sleep or run away and never come back fall into this realm.

Inner vows become bindings and strongholds against emotional closeness. Inner vows create defense mechanisms. Inner vows create a stony heart. Inner vows empower the enemy to work in your life and even bring a curse on you. Ask the Holy Spirit to reveal to you any vows you made with the enemy, knowingly or unknowingly, then renounce them, repent for them, and break the power of them in your life.

PRAY *for* THOSE WHO PERSECUTE YOU

In the Sermon on the Mount Jesus said, "Love your enemies, bless those who curse you, do good to those who hate you, and pray for those who spitefully use you and persecute you, that you may be sons of your Father in heaven. For He makes His sun rise on the evil and on the good and sends rain on the just and on the unjust" (Matt. 5:44–45).

So, what does this look like in action? How do you love your enemies, bless those who curse you, and do good to those who hate you, practically speaking? How do you pray for those who purposefully, knowingly use and abuse you? How do you act like a son or daughter of your Father in heaven? Here are five ways to pray for those who persecute you.

1. Pray that God would forgive them. Although it's vital that you forgive your persecutors, you walk the way Jesus walked when you pray for God to forgive your enemies. Both Jesus and Stephen, while they were being persecuted by enemies of the gospel, prayed that God would forgive their persecutors for their actions. Jesus prayed, "Father, forgive them, for they know not what they do" (Luke 23:34), and Stephen prayed, "Lord, do not hold this sin against them" (Acts 7:60). If you want to be more Christlike, pray as Christ prayed when He was persecuted.

2. Pray for God to give them a spirit of wisdom and revelation in the knowledge of Jesus. Obviously your

persecutors need a greater revelation of Jesus, because the more you truly know Christ, the less you will allow the devil to influence your thoughts, words, and deeds. Pray "that the God of our Lord Jesus Christ, the Father of glory, may give [them] the Spirit of wisdom and revelation in the knowledge of Him, that the eyes of [their] understanding may be enlightened, that [they] may know what is the hope of His calling and what are the riches of the glory of His inheritance among the saints, and what is the surpassing greatness of His power toward us who believe, according to the working of His mighty power" (Eph. 1:17–19).

3. Pray for God to root them and ground them in love. Love is kind (1 Cor. 13:4), but whoever slanders is a fool (Prov. 10:18). The Bible doesn't have anything good to say about fools, but God still loves them—and if they were rooted and grounded in the love of God, they would not gossip, slander, or persecute people. Pray that they, "being rooted and grounded in love, may be able to comprehend with all the saints what is the breadth and length and depth and height, and to know the love of Christ which surpasses knowledge; that [they] may be filled with all the fullness of God" (Eph. 3:17–19).

4. Pray for God's love to abound in them. You can't walk out the Beatitudes without abounding in love. Pray that your persecutors' "love may abound yet more and more in knowledge and in all discernment, that [they] may approve things that are excellent so that [they] may be pure and blameless for the day of Christ, being filled with the fruit of righteousness, which comes through Jesus Christ, for the glory and praise of God" (Phil. 1:9–11).

5. Pray for God to show them His will. Once your persecutors are rooted and grounded in love and understand
   God's will, they will be more likely to repent. Pray that
   they "may be filled with the knowledge of His will in all
   wisdom and spiritual understanding; that [they] may
   walk in a manner worthy of the Lord, pleasing to all,
   being fruitful in every good work, and increasing in the
   knowledge of God" (Col. 1:9–10).

Spiritual Warfare Tactic 81

ASK *the* LORD IF THIS IS YOUR BATTLE *to* FIGHT

Shall I go up?" (2 Sam. 5:19). There is wisdom in asking the same question David did before we run headlong into battle. "Shall I go up?" Every spiritual warrior needs to ask this question before engaging the enemy. We need to be led by the Holy Spirit when we are facing a battle if we want God to lead us into triumph. When we fight a battle the Holy Spirit didn't lead us into in the first place, we are setting ourselves up to lose the battle.

David was a mighty warrior for God. He officially started his military career by defeating a giant named Goliath who terrified the entire Israeli army. (See 1 Samuel 17.) Talk about coming onto the warfare scene with a flare! David built quite a reputation for warfare. In fact, after David defeated Goliath, Saul set the brave teenager over his men of war. When David was coming home from his big win, the women came out of all the cities of Israel. They were singing and dancing and said, "Saul has slain his thousands, and David his ten thousands" (1 Sam. 18:7).

David could have gotten puffed up in the midst of the honor. He could have taken pride in his hand-to-hand combat skills. But he didn't get prideful, and he didn't get presumptuous. And soon enough David had the opportunity to play hero again when the Philistines were fighting against the city of Keilah and robbing the threshing floors (1 Sam. 23:1). Clearly there was an injustice under way, but David didn't take it upon himself to bring justice. Rather, he asked his just God this critical question: "'Shall I go and attack these Philistines?' And the LORD said to David, 'Go and attack the Philistines, and rescue Keilah'" (v. 2).

When David's men admitted they were afraid to go to battle, he wasn't prideful and presumptuous enough to think he could save the whole city with a sling and a stone just because he did it once before. And he didn't pooh-pooh their fears. Instead, David inquired of the Lord a second time. The Lord gave David the confirmation he was looking for: "And the LORD answered him and said, 'Arise, go down to Keilah because I am giving the Philistines into your hand.' Then David and his men went to Keilah. He fought with the Philistines and carried off their livestock, and he struck them with a great slaughter. So David rescued the inhabitants of Keilah" (vv. 4–5).

There's a good lesson here. Even though God initially told David to go up, he was cautious—and humble—enough to continue seeking the Lord for confirmation when it appeared the circumstances could be changing. He was concerned for the welfare of his men, who were afraid. Instead of rebuking them for flowing in fear, he went back to the Lord to make sure he heard right.

I believe this careful, caring approach is one of the reasons David's men trusted his leadership so much. If you want to be an effective general in God's army, you need to pray about your team's legitimate concerns before heading into battle. That doesn't mean you cower in the face of a challenge. It just means you make doubly—even triply—sure that you are in God's will and that you've counted the costs of waging war before leading others into dangerous territory.

Before you run to the battle line, ask the Holy Spirit, "Shall I go up?" Then obey what He tells you. It could be He has assigned someone else to "go up" and defeat the enemy. It could be that God is taking the battle into His own hands. Or it could be that you aren't yet skilled enough in battle to take on the enemy that's rising up. The reason doesn't matter. What matters is being in the will of God, even in our spiritual warfare.

Spiritual Warfare Tactic 82

ACT LIKE *the* PERSISTENT WIDOW

THERE ARE MANY reasons why you may not be receiving victory in your battle, from doubt in your heart (Rom. 10:9) to unconfessed sin (Isa. 59:1–2) to unforgiveness (Mark 11:25) to strife on the home front (1 Pet. 3:7) to turning away from Scripture (Prov. 28:9).

If you've checked your heart in all those areas, consider Jesus's promise: "Ask and it will be given to you; seek and you will find; knock and it will be opened to you. For everyone who asks receives, and he who seeks finds, and to him who knocks, it will be opened" (Matt. 7:7–8). Most Bible translators didn't do us any favors with this rendition because it suggests a single request will get the job done. Especially in the realm of spiritual warfare, sometimes it takes persistent faith to withstand the onslaught in prayer.

That's why I like how the Amplified Bible, Classic Edition translates Matthew 7:7–8: "Keep on asking and it will be given you; keep on seeking and you will find; keep on knocking [reverently] and [the door] will be opened to you. For everyone who keeps on asking receives; and he who keeps on seeking finds; and to him who keeps on knocking, [the door] will be opened."

Ask for victory. Seek Him for strategies. Knock on His door until He answers. Indeed, in the context of Matthew 7, *knocking* means "importunity in dealing with God."[1] That suggests urgent and persistent requests.

Consider the parable of the persistent widow. Jesus used the parable to teach that you should always pray and not lose heart. Jesus also showed that the widow did more than ask: she kept on asking, kept on seeking, and kept on knocking. Read the parable and see this with your own eyes:

> "There was in a certain city a judge who did not fear God nor regard man. Now there was a widow in that city; and she came to him, saying, 'Get justice for me from my adversary.' And he would not for a while; but afterward he said within himself, 'Though I do not fear God nor regard man, yet because this widow troubles me I will avenge her, lest by her continual coming she weary me.'"
>
> Then the Lord said, "Hear what the unjust judge said. And shall God not avenge His own elect who cry out day and night to Him, though He bears long with them? I tell you that He will avenge them speedily. Nevertheless, when the Son of Man comes, will He really find faith on the earth?"
>
> —LUKE 18:2–8, NKJV

When you face opposition to walking through the doorway of promise, when spiritual warfare arises over your stance on the written Word of God or a prophetic word you received, ask God to show you what to do to position yourself for the manifestation, then take any God-inspired action (seek) to find the doorway He leads you to. Once you find the door, start knocking and keep knocking. God will surely open it at the appointed time. Amen.

Spiritual Warfare Tactic 83

OVERCOME EVIL
WITH GOOD

If the weapons of your warfare are not carnal, if they are mighty in God for pulling down strongholds as Paul described in 2 Corinthians 10:4, then forgiveness may be among your stealthiest weapons. The enemy never sees it coming. Think about it for a minute. God used forgiveness to deliver you from the enemy's camp.

When you walk in forgiveness toward others, the enemy cannot put you into bondage to resentment, bitterness, and unforgiveness. When you look at forgiveness through this lens, it becomes a powerful weapon that keeps your heart free and clean. Indeed, obeying God's command to forgive opens the door for God to "punish all disobedience" that caused you harm (2 Cor. 10:6).

Forgiveness is a double-edged sword. If you do not forgive others, God will not forgive you (Matt. 6:15). Unforgiveness hinders your fellowship with God and affects your anointing. You may still command devils in the name of Jesus, but authentic spiritual authority is diluted when you fail to obey God's command to love people. Love and unforgiveness do not flow from the same spring.

If you do not forgive, it will hinder your prayer life. Jesus said, "Whenever you stand praying, if you have anything against anyone, forgive him, that your Father in heaven may also forgive you your trespasses" (Mark 11:25, NKJV). Spiritual warfare falls under the umbrella of prayer. How can you effectively bind devils when you yourself are bound with unforgiveness? Unforgiveness puts you at a clear disadvantage on the spiritual battlefield.

Spiritual warfare is more than binding devils in Jesus's name. Spiritual warfare is forgiving those who oppose you, hurt you, or persecute you. And not only forgiving but blessing. And not only blessing but trusting God to avenge you.

In the Sermon on the Mount, Jesus offered revelation on how to deal with people who mistreat you: "I say to you, love your enemies, bless those who curse you, do good to those who hate you, and pray for those who spitefully use you and persecute you, that you may be sons of your Father who is in heaven" (Matt. 5:44–45). How can you apply that revelation if you aren't willing to forgive?

Paul wrote, "Beloved, do not avenge yourselves, but rather give place to God's wrath, for it is written, 'Vengeance is Mine. I will repay,' says the Lord. Therefore 'If your enemy is hungry, feed him; if he is thirsty, give him a drink; for in so doing you will heap coals of fire on his head.' Do not be overcome by evil, but overcome evil with good" (Rom. 12:19–21).

You may not feel like forgiving. You may feel like giving that someone a piece of your mind. You may not feel like blessing your enemy. You may feel like telling the whole town what he did. You may not feel like showing kindness. You may feel like putting your wrath on display. But when you do, you give the enemy a toehold, which can lead to a foothold, which can lead to a stronghold.

The weapon of forgiveness is mighty not only to pull down strongholds, but to prevent the enemy from establishing a stronghold in the first place. Indeed, forgiveness is a powerful weapon—one that is too often neglected in our binding and loosing exercises. So before you head to the battlefield, consider that "the Lord is long-suffering and slow to anger, and abundant in mercy and lovingkindness, forgiving iniquity and transgression" (Num. 14:18, AMPC).

Spiritual Warfare Tactic 84

BIND
RETALIATION

W E SEE A clear tactic of the enemy throughout Scripture: retaliation. In the Old Testament, Jezebel's children wreaked as much havoc on the kingdom of Israel after her death as the wicked queen did during her reign. Many years after David defeated Goliath, we find four of the giant's descendants intent on taking revenge (2 Sam. 21:18–22).

In the New Testament we see Luke describe the enemy's strategy. After Jesus was tempted in the wilderness for forty days, we read: "When the devil had ended all the temptations, he departed from Him until another time" (Luke 4:13). The NIV describes it as "an opportune time." The NLT says the devil waited "until the next opportunity came." The KJV says "he departed from him for a season." And Young's Literal Translation says the devil "departed from him till a convenient season."

That convenient season was likely when Jesus was in the Garden of Gethsemane. The Bible does not expressly say that Satan was tempting Him, but we know He was battling in His mind because He asked the Lord three times to let the cup of suffering pass from Him, and we know He sweat drops of blood from the pressure. (See Matthew 26:36–44; Luke 22:39–44.)

Although no weapon formed against God's spiritual warriors can prosper, the enemy nonetheless forms a weapon and takes his best shot. After all, when you take a stand against darkness, when you thwart the enemy's plans, you just did marked damage to the kingdom of darkness.

Know this: the enemy will retaliate. He always does. The enemy's retaliation can come immediately after a spiritual victory, and many times it does. But sometimes demon powers wait until the most opportune time—when you least expect it—to strike back. Seasoned spiritual warriors expect the immediate backlash and are on guard for it, but the enemy will often wait until the warrior is in a weakened state physically or emotionally to retaliate.

When you do battle, don't fear the enemy's retaliation. Fear opens the door to enemy attack. He wants you to fear his retaliation. Often he will whisper threats to your heart to intimidate you. Don't fall for it. Instead of fearing the retaliation, become the retaliation. Instead of walking in a defensive posture, go on the offense and stay there.

After every war, bind retaliation in the name of Jesus. Then walk in peace. If the enemy does come to try to repay you for the black eye you gave him, hit him a second time and keep walking in your victory.

DECLARE GOD'S VINDICATING POWER

No WEAPON THAT is formed against you shall prosper, and every tongue that shall rise against you in judgment, you shall condemn. This is the inheritance of the servants of the LORD, and their vindication is from Me, says the LORD" (Isa. 54:17). This is one of my life verses. It reminds me that I have victory. It also reminds me I should not take vindication into my own hands—but leave it in God's hands.

When I am wronged, I declare God's vindicating power and rejoice. See, I've learned the enemy will try to get us to retaliate against those who wronged us or lied about us. The enemy will always tempt us to defend ourselves against obnoxious gossip and slander. The right move is to bless and declare God's vindicating power.

Paul admonishes us: "Beloved, do not avenge yourselves, but rather give place to God's wrath, for it is written: 'Vengeance is Mine. I will repay,' says the Lord" (Rom. 12:19). And again, "See that no one renders evil for evil to anyone. But always seek to do good to one another and to all" (1 Thess. 5:15). And Peter tells us, "Do not repay evil for evil, or curse for curse, but on the contrary, bless, knowing that to this you are called, so that you may receive a blessing" (1 Pet. 3:9).

In His teaching about revenge in the Sermon on the Mount, Jesus said, "You have heard that it was said, 'An eye for an eye, and a tooth for a tooth.' But I say to you, do not resist an evil person. But whoever strikes you on your right cheek, turn to him the other as well. And if anyone sues you in a court of law and takes away your tunic, let him have your cloak also. And whoever compels you to go one mile, go with him two. Give to him who asks you, and from him who would borrow from you do not turn away" (Matt. 5:38–42).

In all cases it is better not to defend yourself but instead to allow God to defend you. At times you may need to make a public explanation, but offering a statement in the right spirit is different than being defensive. As long as you are bent on defending yourself, you are tying God's hands.

Isaiah 35:4 encourages us to "be strong, fear not. Your God will come with vengeance, even God with a recompense; He will come and save you." Psalm 135:14 assures us, "The LORD will defend His people, and He will have compassion on His servants."

When the enemy works against you, either directly through assaults on your mind and body or through people who wrong you, declare God's vindicating power and pray for those who hurt you. Then pray for God's vindication against the spirits at work behind the scenes and, again, for mercy on anyone the enemy is using against you. Psalm 94:1 gives us an example: "O LORD God, to whom vengeance belongs; O God to whom vengeance belongs, shine forth." Put it in His hands, and you will be among those who say, "Surely there is a reward for the righteous; surely there is a God who judges on the earth" (Ps. 58:11).

Spiritual Warfare Tactic 86

SURRENDER
EVERYTHING *to* GOD

WHETHER YOU ARE in ministry, in the marketplace, or tackling the all-important task of raising a family—or perhaps, like me, doing all three at the same time—you will no doubt come to a point in your walk with God when you feel like giving up because of the intensity of the warfare.

The answer is not to give up. The answer is to surrender—and there's a vast difference between the two. *Merriam-Webster* defines the word *surrender* as "to yield to the power, control, or possession of another upon compulsion or demand; to give up completely or agree to forgo especially in favor of another."[1]

Deny your instinct to fight the battle in your own strength and surrender to His wisdom. Deny the temptation to give up and surrender to the power that raised Christ from the dead and dwells in you to overcome the enemy. Deny your feelings of frustration and surrender to His grace.

Surrender your anger for His peace. Surrender your intellect, reasonings, and imaginations for His discernment. Surrender everything you have and everything you are to God's will. When Jesus was in the Garden of Gethsemane, He demonstrated the art of surrender in the midst of intense spiritual pressure. Consider the scene in Mark 14:33–36:

> He took Peter and James and John with Him and began to be greatly distressed and very troubled. And He said to them, "My soul is deeply sorrowful unto death. Remain here and keep watch." He went a little farther and fell on the ground and prayed that, if it were possible, the hour

might pass from Him. He said, "Abba, Father, all things are possible for You. Remove this cup from Me; yet not what I will, but what You will."

Part of surrendering is putting on the altar dreams, visions, objects, and people over which the enemy is battling. When you can't discern the perfect will of the Lord in a thing—when you aren't sure if the Lord is calling you to fight or let it go, but the war is raging against you nonetheless—learn to surrender by putting everything on the altar.

You can pray like this:

> Father, I don't know what's going on. I don't know what to do. I surrender to You, and I surrender everything I have to You. I put this on the altar. I put my calling on the altar. I put my life on the altar. Lord, give back to me what You want me to have. Take away what You don't want me to have.

Surrender is a keen spiritual warfare strategy because at times you're fighting the devil for things you aren't supposed to have in the first place. Therefore, you're fighting senseless battles you can never really win. When you put everything on the altar in complete surrender to His will, you can trust Him to show you what's worth fighting for and what you need to sacrifice. Just as the angel stayed Abraham's hand from slaying Isaac, the promised son, on the altar (Gen. 22:2–14), God will not allow anything in His will to be consumed with fire. And sometimes God just wants to see that you will keep Him first when you get the promise.

Spiritual Warfare Tactic 87

CHRONICLE YOUR WARFARE *in a* JOURNAL

JOURNALING IS A powerful tool for spiritual warriors. There is absolutely no way you can remember everything about your battle—every stumble, every feeling, every voice, every weapon that worked, every support player in the war—without journaling. The Bible is full of chronicles of war.

Journaling is vital because, doubtless, there will be moments in time you chronicle with your own pen and paper—or digital keyboard—that will be vital for debriefing. (Debriefing is another warfare tactic we'll discuss later in the book that empowers you for the next skirmish.)

Indeed, journaling helps you remember the good, the bad, and the ugly from the battle. Journaling gives you a safe place to vent thoughts and feelings that are best kept between you and God, but which you may want to remember later as you review how the enemy tripped you or how God specifically spoke to your heart.

God told Jeremiah, "Write all the words that I have spoken to you in a book" (Jer. 30:2). When you write down what the Lord tells you in the midst of the battle, you'll have more confidence after the victory that you followed His battle plan. What's more, you may forget what He told you amid the chaos in your soul. Writing down what the Lord has said helps you stay steady in the spiritual fray because you can go back and read it again and again to build your faith amid demonic attacks.

Psalm 119:27 tells us, "Make me to understand the way of Your precepts; then I shall contemplate on Your wondrous works." When you record your victories in battle, you can more easily put yourself in remembrance of God's faithfulness in the last battle. You can read through your weak moments and see how God proved the reality of Romans 8:28—that He works all things together for the good of those who love Him and are called according to His purposes.

Journaling can even bring healing from battle wounds. Psychologists have discussed the concept of freeing the mind from trauma by dumping it out on paper. Call it an emotional release—journaling can relieve the stress of the war.

Especially while the battle is raging, using your journal to express gratitude and praise is strategic. Gratitude journals have become a popular item in bookstores. But you don't have to buy a fancy book to write down what you are grateful for each day. Pour out in your journal not just your sorrows but your praise, adoration, and thanksgiving to God.

Before you start journaling each day, pray to God for inspiration—that His wisdom may come through your pen while you write. Put on some worship music. Have your Bible nearby. Journal scriptures that apply to your situation and meditate on them.

Remember, journaling chronicles the enemy's plots and plans against your life so that you grow from the experience. But ultimately you are chronicling God's victorious hand in your life—and your change and growth as He morphs you into the image of His dear Son.

REMEMBER PEOPLE ARE NOT YOUR ENEMY

The BIBLE SAYS we are not wrestling against flesh and blood, but against demon forces (Eph. 6:12). Of course, that doesn't mean people don't act like the devil sometimes. Indeed, it sure feels at times as if people are our enemy.

After all, when our coworkers gossip about us, slander us, and try to make us look bad in front of the boss, they are the ones flapping their jaws. When companies cheat and steal from us, they are the ones seemingly gaining from the theft while our pocketbooks are dented. When family members or friends stab us in the back, they are the ones holding the proverbial knife. When people abuse us, they are the ones committing the sin.

Yes, all that is true. The devil himself has not committed these and other horrible acts against us. But oftentimes he is motivating people to behave in an ungodly manner by tapping into the works of the flesh, which include adultery, hatred, strife, envy, and the like (Gal. 5:19–21).

Ultimately the enemy influences people to behave the way they do through the sin nature or through vain imaginations he whispers to their souls. The enemy may tell a coworker you are out to get them, so they seek to get you first. The enemy may tell your spouse you don't appreciate them, so they are seduced into immorality. The enemy may tell someone you can afford to pay a higher price for that car, so they swindle you.

Although people are responsible for their own thoughts, words, and deeds, oftentimes there is an enemy behind the scenes using them as a puppet of sorts to make you miserable. And while many demon-inspired attacks come from absolute strangers, the enemy often uses the people closest to us to provoke us, disappoint us, or flat-out attack us.

If you view people as your enemies, you'll violate the law of love. The Bible tells us to walk in love (Eph. 5:2). The Bible tells us faith works by love (Gal. 5:6). The Bible tells us to love our enemies (Luke 6:27). Yes, people can act like our enemies at times and, in some sense, we may find we have "enemies." But when we walk in love with those who are walking in the wrong against us, we're acting like our Father in heaven (Matt. 5:43–48).

When it seems like people are your enemies—when they are acting like enemies—take on the mind-set of the psalmist: "For the mouth of the wicked and deceitful are opened against me; they have spoken against me with a lying tongue. They encircled me with words of hatred and fought against me without cause. In return for my love they are my adversaries, but I give myself to prayer" (Ps. 109:2–4).

Remember people are not your enemy.

DON'T BEAT
the AIR

Paul the apostle was an efficient spiritual warrior. He described himself this way: "So, therefore, I run, not with uncertainty. So I fight, not as one who beats the air" (1 Cor. 9:26). The NLT translates this concept as "shadowboxing."

While one name for Satan is the "prince of the power of the air" (Eph. 2:2), Paul was not flailing his arms wildly in the spirit hoping he might hit something—and neither should we. Paul wasn't shadowboxing—that is, sparring with an imaginary opponent as part of his spiritual training. He wasn't having slugfest based on assumptions.

Likewise, Paul didn't blindfold himself and shoot an arrow hoping it would hit his target. The apostle may not have seen his enemies with his natural eyes, but he certainly discerned them with his spiritual senses.

Think about it for a minute. Paul spoke of wrestling beasts at Ephesus (1 Cor. 15:32). He wasn't referring to wild animals; he was talking about spiritual beings. He tells us plainly in Ephesians 6:12 that "our fight is not against flesh and blood, but against principalities, against powers, against the rulers of the darkness of this world, and against spiritual forces of evil in the heavenly places." David fought the lion and the bear. Paul fought the principalities and powers.

Much the same, Paul knew the spirit that was attacking him when he cast the devil out of a girl in Thyatira. Let's look at the account:

On one occasion, as we went to the place of prayer, a servant girl possessed with a spirit of divination met us, who brought her masters much profit by fortune-telling. She followed Paul and us, shouting, "These men are servants of the Most High God, who proclaim to us the way of salvation." She did this for many days. But becoming greatly troubled, Paul turned to the spirit and said, "I command you in the name of Jesus Christ to come out of her." And it came out at that moment.

—ACTS 16:16–18

Many times spirits will not immediately bow, flee, or come out if you do not name them specifically. I don't completely understand why. What I do know is if you start swinging wildly—beating the air, as Paul puts it—you will likely hit a spirit that wasn't intent on hitting you. If you play guessing games in the spirit, hoping that one of the spirits you call out might be accurate, you are asking for retaliation. You don't want to stir up devils that are not assigned to you.

In the realm of spiritual warfare you want to develop and maintain accuracy in the spirit. Rather than a buckshot approach, rifling off the name of one spirit after another after another and hoping to hit the unseen enemy that has set you in its crosshairs, you want to identify and hit your target on the first shot if possible. Like a sharpshooter, you want to develop spiritual skills that make you a master marksman with precise aim at short range and long range.

Spiritual Warfare Tactic 90

DEAL WITH DEMONS FROM YOUR PAST

M<small>ANY</small> <small>BELIEVERS</small> <small>HAVE</small> dramatic testimonies of how God delivered them from dark places into which even your typical sinner doesn't venture. But if you aren't truly free from the demonic influences that held you in bondage, you could fall back into the snare of the enemy once again. You are forgiven from your past sins, but sometimes you must deal with your past demons.

Your position in Christ is clearly spelled out in the Word of God, but that doesn't mean when you got saved, you were immediately delivered from demons of the past that plagued your soul. If you don't deal with the demons from your past, the devil will come at a more opportune time and try to steal, kill, and destroy.

Demons from the past are often recognizable as persistent issues that hold you back from God's best. When you encounter one, it is like hitting a wall you can't leap over, get around, dig under, or break through. It's a bondage. Often deliverance ministry is required, but even then you have to do your part. It is spiritual warfare from the inside out rather than the outside in. In other words, you aren't battling external forces only; you are battling demons that have found residence in your soul.

The Holy Spirit is faithful to bring to your attention the issues that you need to deal with, if you don't already see them. He may do that one-on-one or use a trusted person in your life to point out a problem in love. When you can see a demonic stronghold, whether subtly in your thoughts or fully manifest through your actions, you need to get help.

So how do you deal with demons from your past? Acknowledge

that there is a problem. Confront it courageously. Stop running from it. Don't deny it's there. Don't try to build your walls higher. Take off the mask you've been using to disguise the pain you are going through.

That requires humility, but humility opens the door to God's grace. Get some help from trusted Christians in your life who are equipped to help you find the deliverance and healing you need in Christ. Don't worry about what other people are going to think if they know the truth. If they are discerning people, they probably already know you are struggling. Where you find yourself may not be your fault, but getting free requires you to take responsibility for your choices now.

The same old emotions may continue to come even after you deal with the demons of your past. But when Jesus sets you free by the power of the Holy Ghost, you are free indeed (John 8:36). Once you confront the demons from your past, you will gain a new perspective. When those old emotions, old thoughts, and old temptations come rolling back around, you will be able to recognize what is happening and respond rather than reacting to the demon's taunt.

As you continue to do this, you will build your spiritual muscles and eventually the demon will give up and go bother someone else. God will meet you at the point of your decision and help you overcome the demons of your past. Victory belongs to you. Decide to walk in it.

AVOID SPIRITUAL WARFARE EXTREMES

As a young Christian I was raised in spiritual warfare. My church home was akin to a spiritual war zone. We were always on red alert through prophetic warnings, dreams, and visions about the next attack. Indeed, spiritual warfare was a consistent thread in most of the praise, worship, equipping classes, Sunday morning sermons, and leadership lessons.

You might call it "extreme apostolic." We hunted down the demon(s) behind every doorknob like a child with a sweet tooth hunts for chocolate Easter eggs. Looking back, it seemed at times like a contest to determine who could present the most detailed dream or vision about the enemy's impending plan. Once the enemy was spotted, a shouting match with the principality or power ensued that left you with a sore throat—and no respite from the warfare.

I was in an extreme spiritual warfare ditch, where the enemy and his plans were ultimately exalted over God and His plans. Don't get me wrong. I believe wholeheartedly in spiritual warfare. But we can get into a ditch with any principle if we take it to the extreme. So we have to ask ourselves: What causes us to take biblical principles to the extreme?

There's no single answer, but we can guard ourselves from deception by adding balance and soberness of mind to our vigilance. Our enemy is roaming around like a lion, seeking someone to seize upon and devour (1 Pet. 5:8), and getting out of balance opens a door wide enough for him to freely enter.

Then again, it could be possible that you are in a completely different ditch. Maybe you aren't going on the offense against the devil at all. Maybe you aren't doing your part to protect your spiritual garden from demonic weeds. The problem is, God won't do our part for us. He's given us authority in this earth realm. He's done all He's going to do about the devil. Jesus gave us His authority, as well as keys to the kingdom. Whatever we bind on earth is bound in heaven, and whatever we loose on earth is loosed in heaven (Matt. 16:19). In other words, we can't blame God when the devil gets in. We're the ones who allow it.

Again, I started out in an extreme spiritual warfare ditch, where even worship music was an exercise in combat. Yet having escaped a church where strife ruled and reigned—and in which Jezebel was typically blamed for most of the rumblings in the congregation—I entered a prophetic church that took an opposite approach. And I entered another spiritual warfare ditch.

During my extended season at this prophetic church, I never heard them bind Jezebel once—not even once. I never heard anyone come against witchcraft or rebuke the spirit of religion. All they did was praise and worship the Lord for hours on end and roll around on the floor and laugh. This was unusual for me, perhaps especially so after exiting the extreme apostolic. It was actually refreshing. I enjoyed it—until I got blindsided by the enemy and realized I was in another ditch.

After living in both extremes, I have learned a lesson: we must all become skilled warriors and intimate worshippers. In doing so, we avoid either ditch of extremism and walk in the discernment of the Holy Ghost, knowing when to run to the battle line and knowing when to worship.

DISCERN
SPIRITUAL CLIMATES

T HE SPIRITUAL CLIMATE in a region is affected by the spiritual activity in a region. You can drill this down even further to your workplace, your home, or any environment.

What is a spiritual climate? In our context we can rely on the *Merriam-Webster* definition of *climate*: "the prevailing set of conditions (as of temperature and humidity) indoors; the prevailing influence or environmental conditions characterizing a group or period."[1]

You may have heard people speak of a climate of fear or a climate of suspicion. The idea here is that you can pick up on the prevailing influence or set of conditions in any given place through your physical and spiritual senses. When I walk into health food stores, for example, I often pick up on a New Age climate due to the products sold in the store and the people who shop there. When I walk into a church, I can quickly discern if the climate is friendly to the Holy Spirt or if a religious spirit prevails.

Let me give you a practical example: Have you ever been in a church service where everyone was hungry for God and worshipping Him with all their heart, mind, soul, and strength? The presence of God so fills the sanctuary that some start weeping. Perhaps others lie on their face on the floor. Still others just hold up their hands in awe and continue praising His name. Worshipping God in spirit and truth shifts the spiritual atmosphere. With so many believers in one accord, the King of glory, the Lord strong and mighty, manifests His presence in a special way.

By contrast, when people are worshipping evil or pressing into occult practices of any type, it affects the spiritual climate in a city. You empower what you worship, but ultimately witchcraft or Jezebel or gambling or lust or divorce or fear are not the principalities over your city. Jesus, the King of kings, the Lord of lords, the Prince of Peace, is the principality over your city. He is ruler. Still, principalities and powers do affect the spiritual atmosphere when they are allowed to freely operate.

When you are in a hard spiritual climate, it can seem like your prayers hit a bronze ceiling and fall back down to the earth again. Of course, we know that's not true because God hears the prayers of the righteous (Prov. 15:29). But prayer often feels like a heated battle when you are in a tight spiritual climate with demonic strongholds. Sometimes you don't even feel like praying.

When demonic activity is rising in a city, a sensitive Christian will discern it. Unless you know what is operating, you will think the imaginations against your mind are you, or the fatigue is natural because you get up so early, or the feelings of giving up are legitimate because of the long trial you've endured.

The Word of God says, "My people are destroyed for lack of knowledge" (Hosea 4:6). I've discovered again and again that when I share the revelation on spiritual climates, this truth sets people free to submit themselves to God and resist the devil so he'll flee. Ask the Lord to make you sensitive to His heart and to make you aware of the spiritual climate around you so you can be spiritually ready for the battle that may ensue.

REMEMBER YOU'RE NOT FIGHTING ALONE

SOMETIMES THE SPIRITUAL warfare just seems to come from all sides. Sometimes it seems to come from all sides at once. Sometimes in the midst of the onslaught it feels like you are fighting alone. And sometimes you really are battling without a prayer partner who could help put an additional nine thousand demons to flight (Deut. 32:30).

Paul once told his spiritual son Timothy: "At my first defense no one stood with me, but everyone forsook me. May it not be charged against them" (2 Tim. 4:16). Elijah was convinced he was fighting alone. He once told the Israelites, "I alone remain a prophet of the LORD, but Baal's prophets number four hundred fifty men" (1 Kings 18:22). And after defeating the false prophets on Mount Carmel, twice Elijah told the Lord, "I alone am left, and they seek to take my life" (1 Kings 19:10, 14).

David knew what it was like to fight alone. He fought the lion alone. He fought the bear alone. And he was the only one among the Israelites who wasn't afraid to stand up to Goliath alone (1 Sam. 17). Some of David's mighty men also knew what it felt like to fight alone. After the men of Israel retreated, Eleazar arose and attacked the Philistines until his hand was stuck to the sword (2 Sam. 23:9–10). Can you imagine? Another time, when the Israelites fled from the Philistines, Shammah stationed himself in the middle of a field of lentils the enemy was looking to occupy. He defended it and killed the Philistines all by himself (vv. 11–12).

Sometimes you may be fighting alone. But many times it just feels like you are standing solo. Elijah, for example, had a wrong perception of the warfare. He was on the run from Jezebel and her witchcraft. She released a word curse over him carrying fear that struck his heart (1 Kings 19:2). He left his servant, who likely would have warred with him, behind and went into hiding. These are the moves of one weary from battle who feels he is fighting alone. But the Lord set Elijah straight: "Still, I have preserved seven thousand men in Israel for Myself, all of whose knees have not bowed to Baal and whose mouths have not kissed him" (1 Kings 19:18). Friends, you may be fighting your battle alone, but remember that the Lord has many others who are also taking a stand for righteousness.

When you feel as if you are fighting alone, pray for all those who are going through a similar battle and have no one to stand in the gap for them. In other words, get your focus off yourself and intercede for someone else. God can move on a total stranger's heart to intercede for you.

Some days it may feel as if you are fighting alone. From a natural perspective, you may be. But the Lord is faithful. This battle is ultimately the Lord's, and when you stand for Him—and when all hell breaks loose against you for that stance—He will strengthen you! He will anoint you! He will deliver you! He will preserve you! Amen!

BIND *the* STRONGMAN

I N EVERY BATTLE there's a strongman. Identifying the strongman and binding him is a key to plundering his house and taking back what belongs to you. Jesus explains: "When a strong man, fully armed, guards his own palace, his goods are peacefully kept. But when a stronger man than he attacks and overpowers him, he seizes all the armor in which the man trusted and divides his spoils" (Luke 11:21–22).

In this verse Satan is the "strongman" and Jesus is the "stronger man." In the context of spiritual warfare, though, most people never stand face-to-face with Satan. Satan deploys one of his demons to serve as the strongman in proxy. The strongman could be the spirit of fear, the spirit of poverty, the spirit of Jezebel, or any other spirit on assignment. Many demons may line up in battle formation against you, but the strongman is behind the front line, hoping you don't see him. Ask the Lord for discernment as to what the strongman is, then set your sights on binding him with the authority you carry in Jesus's name.

Ephesians 6:10 tells us to "be strong in the Lord." This is a vital scripture to meditate upon if you set out to bind the strongman in any battle. Remember, it's by the Lord's power that you can bind the devil. We cannot fight any demon power in our own strength. As Zechariah 4:6 says, "Not by might nor by power, but by My Spirit, says the LORD of Hosts."

When you take your authority to bind the strongman, you are depending on the stronger man's ability to overpower him. In Christ you are a stronger man. The Greek word for stronger in Luke 11:22

is *ischyros*. It means "strong, mighty; strong either in body or in mind; of one who has strength of soul to sustain the attacks of Satan, strong and therefore exhibiting many excellences."[1]

Think of the strongman as a spoiler. There are nineteen references to "spoilers" in the Bible.[2] Spoiler demons work under the John 10:10 mandate to steal, kill, and destroy. Spoilers are plunderers. *Plunder* means "to take the goods of by force (as in war); to take by force or wrongfully."[3] Spoilers invade your territory and pillage what belongs to you, carrying away booty like a pirate at high sea (Ezek. 39:10). Spoilers work in darkness (Obad. 5). Spoilers prey upon you when you are not aware and ravage your treasures (1 Pet. 5:8).

When it comes to spoilers, you don't always see them coming. You pray and watch and hope to discern enemy attacks, but sometimes you get blindsided by one enemy when you're fighting another enemy. Don't lose heart. You can recover all. You can spoil the spoilers with God's battle plan.

The strongman sets up strongholds. But your weapons are "mighty through God for the pulling down of strongholds" that defy God's will in your life (2 Cor. 10:4). Many times you can tear down strongholds, but if you don't bind the strongman, he will reerect those strongholds. Some battles just won't end until you attack and overpower—what some translations render as "bind"—the strongman. When you do, you get the spoils.

Spiritual Warfare Tactic 95

CAST YOUR CARES
on the LORD

THE CARES OF this world can choke the Word of God right out of our hearts. That's dangerous because the Word of God is what sparks faith to fight the good fight. It's hard to fight when we are burdened down with weights. We must learn to not only cast the devil out but also to cast our cares on God.

Indeed, there's a spiritual warfare revelation in 1 Peter I had not fully grasped until recently. I often quote 1 Peter 5:8–9 (AMPC):

> Be well balanced (temperate, sober of mind), be vigilant and cautious at all times; for that enemy of yours, the devil, roams around like a lion roaring [in fierce hunger], seeking someone to seize upon and devour. Withstand him; be firm in faith [against his onset—rooted, established, strong, immovable, and determined], knowing that the same (identical) sufferings are appointed to your brotherhood (the whole body of Christians) throughout the world.

This scripture paints a vivid picture of our adversary. But only by reading the enter chapter from which these verses come do we see the whole picture of how the enemy uses our cares—cares he magnifies so they seem much more troublesome than they actually are—against us. We'll look at verses 5–7, which immediately precede Paul's warning about the devil.

> Clothe (apron) yourselves, all of you, with humility [as the garb of a servant, so that its covering cannot possibly be stripped from you, with freedom from pride and arrogance] toward one another. For God sets Himself against

the proud (the insolent, the overbearing, the disdainful, the presumptuous, the boastful)—[and He opposes, frustrates, and defeats them], but gives grace (favor, blessing) to the humble.

Therefore humble yourselves [demote, lower yourselves in your own estimation] under the mighty hand of God, that in due time He may exalt you, casting the whole of your care [all your anxieties, all your worries, all your concerns, once and for all] on Him, for He cares for you affectionately and cares about you watchfully.

Can you see the connection here? Apart from Jesus we can do nothing (John 15:5). We must live and move and have our being in Him (Acts 17:28). We must lean and depend on Him in everything, especially in trials, tribulations, and spiritual warfare. That requires humility. God gives grace to walk through adversity and to battle the enemy when we humble ourselves.

By contrast, God resists the proud. Pride makes us think we can take care of ourselves—and take care of our cares. Pride tempts us to reason out all the answers instead of waiting on the strategy or intervention of the One who has all the answers. Pride doesn't trust anybody, not even God. God will lift us above our enemies—even prepare a table before us in the presence of our enemies (Ps. 23:5)—when we humble ourselves and cast our cares on Him.

Think about it for a minute. How can we be spiritually alert and heavenly minded when we are carrying cares He told us not to carry? The short answer is, we can't. Jesus Himself said, "Be not careful therefore for the morrow, for the morrow shall be careful about itself. Sufficient to the day [is] its own evil" (Matt. 6:34, DARBY). Cast your cares now and regularly!

OVERCOME DEMONIC OVERWHELM

SOMETIMES LIFE CAN be absolutely overwhelming. The enemy is an expert at coming in like a flood with crushing circumstances and disturbing thoughts that try to drown you in feelings of helplessness and even hopelessness. "Overwhelm" is an enemy I've fought many times over the years, and defeating it starts with understanding what it really is.

Merriam-Webster defines *overwhelm* as "to affect (someone) very strongly; to cause (someone) to have too many things to deal with; to defeat (someone or something) completely; upset, overthrow; to cover over completely; submerge; to overcome by superior force or numbers; to overpower in thought or feeling."[1]

Don't feel ashamed in your battle against overwhelm. David understood these feelings all too well. He once wrote, "My heart is in pain within me, and the terrors of death have fallen on me. Fear and trembling come into me, and horror has overwhelmed me. I said, 'Oh, that I had wings like a dove! For then I would fly away and be at rest. Indeed, then I would wander far off, and remain in the wilderness. Selah I would hasten my escape from the windy storm and tempest'" (Ps. 55:4–8).

The first step in battling overwhelm is to recognize it and acknowledge the situation you find yourself in. Denying feelings of overwhelm won't help you conquer your flesh or the devil. Once you've acknowledged the reality of an overwhelmed heart, you can work with the Holy Spirit to get to the root of these feelings.

What is causing this overwhelm, really? Is the enemy blowing it out of proportion? Is it really as bad as it looks, or is this pressure demonic? Put your circumstances and your emotions into perspective. Is there anything you can do right now in the natural to relieve some of the burdens you feel?

Get your mind off the overwhelming circumstances and onto the Word of God. Pray for grace, strength, and whatever else you feel you need from the Father in the moment. Remind yourself of His promises. "From the end of the earth I will cry to You, when my heart is overwhelmed; lead me to the rock that is higher than I" (Ps. 61:2, NKJV).

Remember David. When he was overwhelmed with Saul hunting him down, with Absalom trying to overtake his kingdom, with his baby son dying, and even with his own sin, he always turned to God. Here is one of his prayers for help in troubling times that you may want to pray for yourself:

> I cry aloud with my voice to the LORD; I make supplication with my voice to the LORD. I pour out my complaint before Him; I declare my trouble before Him. When my spirit was overwhelmed within me, You knew my path. In the way where I walk they have hidden a trap for me. Look to the right and see; for there is no one who regards me; there is no escape for me; no one cares for my soul.
>
> I cried out to You, O LORD; I said, "You are my refuge, my portion in the land of the living. Give heed to my cry, for I am brought very low; deliver me from my persecutors, for they are too strong for me. Bring my soul out of prison, so that I may give thanks to Your name; the righteous will surround me, for You will deal bountifully with me."
>
> —PSALM 142, NASB

Spiritual Warfare Tactic 97

BREAK
THOUGHT CURSES

Recently, as I was praying to break word curses, the Holy Spirit reminded me of the reality of thought curses. "Even in your mind do not curse the king; and in your bedchamber do not curse the rich; for a bird in the sky may carry your voice, and a winged creature may declare the matter" (Eccles. 10:20).

The word *curse* in that scripture means "to make despicable; to curse; to make light; to treat with contempt, bring contempt or dishonor."[1] The Bible says not to curse people "even in your mind;" other translations say "in your thoughts" (e.g., AMPC). Even in your mind! A word curse gives voice to an evil thought, but how can a thought take voice in the spirit realm?

When we think wrong thoughts about people—or about ourselves—we're violating Scripture. Paul tells us, "Whatever things are true, whatever things are honest, whatever things are just, whatever things are pure, whatever things are lovely, whatever things are of good report, if there is any virtue, and if there is any praise, think on these things" (Phil. 4:8).

When we are thinking wrong thoughts about people—or ourselves—we are agreeing with the accuser of the brethren. We're getting on the devil's side and allowing him to feed our minds ammunition that will eventually come out of our mouths and become a word curse. Think about it for a minute. If we meditate on how angry and upset we are about people because they wronged us, how long will it be before we speak out those thought curses and transform them into word curses?

As Christians we need to obey Scripture. Second Corinthians

10:5–6 talks about casting down imaginations, but we often forget the part that says to bring "every thought into captivity to the obedience of Christ, and being ready to punish all disobedience when your obedience is complete."

Combatting thought curses starts with our own thoughts. If we're cursing ourselves in our thoughts, we need to intentionally think the opposite of what the enemy is telling us, what people say about us, or what we think about our own shortcomings. We need to declare the truth out of our mouths. By the same token, we need to guard our thoughts about others. We don't want to be used of the enemy against anyone and violate the law of love.

Now, if you discern thought curses are coming against you, move in the Luke 6:28 principle: "bless those who curse you," even if you don't know who they are. Next, bind thought curses and word curses in the name of Jesus with the Matthew 16:19 key. Finally, take authority over every demonic thought that has been formed against your life and gird up the loins of your mind, for that is where the root of the battle really lies.

Spiritual Warfare Tactic 98

SEEK GODLY COUNSEL

WHEN WAR IS raging against your mind, it can be difficult to discern what to do. That's when you need to seek godly counsel. Please make sure it's godly counsel. If you ask the wrong person for advice in the middle of your battle, it may not go well with you. The world's ways, as wise as they may sound in a vulnerable moment, will not bring you victory.

Psalm 1:1–3 says, "Blessed is the man who walks not in the counsel of the ungodly, nor stands in the path of sinners, nor sits in the seat of scoffers; but his delight is in the law of the LORD, and in His law he meditates day and night. He will be like a tree planted by the rivers of water, that brings forth its fruit in its season; its leaf will not wither, and whatever he does will prosper."

Remember, your emotions can betray you. Seek counsel from those who are more experienced in life or more discerning than you. Personally I always seek counsel from various perspectives when I face a problem or need to make an important decision. I hear the voice of the Lord in godly counsel. Godly counsel—that on-time word—always bears witness with my spirit.

The enemy doesn't want you to seek wise, godly counsel because he understands the power inherent in experience. But over and over Scripture admonishes us to seek wise, godly counsel. Proverbs 11:14 tells us, "Where there is no counsel, the people fall; but in the multitude of counselors there is safety." And Proverbs 15:22 says, "Without counsel, purposes are disappointed, but in the multitude of counselors they are established."

Don't allow pride or shame convince you not to seek godly

counsel in warfare. Don't assume the "I can do it myself" attitude when you are already struggling; it's a foolish stance. Proverbs 12:15 tells us, "The way of a fool is right in his own eyes, but he who listens to counsel is wise." Proverbs 28:26 says, "He who trusts in his own heart is a fool, but whoever walks wisely will be delivered."

Be careful not to buck and fight against strategic counsel because it doesn't make sense to you. While I always bear witness to wise counsel, the truth is it doesn't have to make sense to come from God. If what you are doing isn't working, it's time to try a new tactic. You don't know what you don't know, and you can't see what you can't see. Many times others have a clearer perspective.

Proverbs 13:10 warns us, "Only by pride comes contention, but with the well-advised is wisdom." Proverbs 19:20 assures us, "Hear counsel and receive instruction, that you may be wise in your latter days."

The value of godly counsel is a repeated theme in the Book of Proverbs, penned by the man known as the wisest on earth. Solomon wrote, "Every purpose is established by counsel, and with good advice wage war" (Prov. 20:18). He also penned this truth: "For by wise counsel you will wage your war, and in multitude of counselors there is safety" (Prov. 24:6).

DON'T UNDERESTIMATE YOUR ENEMY

It CAN BE quite dangerous to underestimate your enemy. By the same token, don't overestimate your own spiritual warfare skills. And, finally, don't underestimate your God.

Let's focus, though, on the aspect of underestimating the enemy. I've heard many people say, "Oh, the devil is stupid." No, he is not stupid. Satan is a fallen angel, whose name was Lucifer in heaven before he led an insurrection against God Almighty. Created as an angel, Satan has many of the characteristics of angels, but pride perverted them.

Angels were created with an intellect, emotions, and a will. Both angels and demons have intelligence and curiosity (1 Pet. 1:12). Angels and demons have emotions (James 2:19). Angels and demons have a will (2 Tim. 2:26). Angels and demons are people without bodies. Angels and demons know what God has said in His Word (Rev. 12:12).

Moreover, angels and demons have been watching the human race for thousands of years. Demons have more experience waging warfare against humans than any single human will gain on his short time on earth. Demons can often calculate your next move because they have observed how humans respond to pressure, pain, and lies for centuries. Demons are experts at tempting you to sin and then condemning you for sinning. Demons are always on the hunt, waiting for an opportunity to pounce. In his book *The Journey* beloved evangelist Billy Graham put it this way: "Don't think of Satan as a harmless cartoon character with a red suit and a pitchfork. He is very clever and powerful, and his unchanging purpose is to defeat God's plans at every turn—including His plans for your life."[1]

The Bible reveals Satan has power (Luke 10:19). The Bible warns us not to be ignorant of how he operates (2 Cor. 2:11). Make no mistake—Satan and his principalities, powers, rulers of the darkness of this age, and spiritual wickedness in high places are a highly organized army that is unified for one purpose: to destroy God's creation.

The good news is Satan's power is limited. We don't want to overestimate, by any means, his power in our lives. Ultimately he only has the power we give him with our thoughts, words, and deeds. Satan is not all-powerful, he is not all-knowing, and he is not everywhere. God's power, on the other hand, is unlimited. God's knows all things. God sees all things. God is everywhere all the time—and He is with us.

With all this in mind, we don't want to overestimate the enemy's ability to bring destruction in our lives and walk in fear. Fear opens the door to attack. Read the Bible and study how the enemy works, but spend more time worshipping the Lord. Don't ignore the devil or his abilities, but spend more time thinking about Father, Son, and Holy Spirit than you do about principalities, powers, and demons. And don't underestimate yourself. You are more than a conqueror in Christ (Rom. 8:37).

DEBRIEF AFTER
the BATTLE

W HEN THE BATTLE is over, don't just resume life as usual as
if nothing happened. Many times after a severe battle you are so
relieved the pressure is off, you are tempted to move on and not
look back. But that's not the right move strategically.

With Bible, pen, and paper, take some time to reflect on what
you've just experienced. Determine to learn anything and everything you can about yourself, your God, and your enemy in the
aftermath of the warfare. Don't miss this opportunity to glean valuable insights about how the enemy operates, how you responded
for better or worse, and how your God came through. Assess who
really stood with you in the serious storm.

I call this debriefing after the battle. It's akin to what the military does after a solider returns from war. *Merriam-Webster*
defines *debrief* as "to carefully review upon completion." Another
definition is "to interrogate (someone, such as a pilot) usually upon
return (as from a mission) in order to obtain useful information."[1]

In this case, you're interrogating yourself and, in a sense, interrogating God. You are examining and recording what the enemy
did in your life that was effective so you can shore up those weak
areas in your soul. You are recording what instructions God gave
to you, if any, in the heat of the battle that led to victory. You are
considering your thoughts and actions, for better or worse.

While you are debriefing, it's also important to look at what
you did right. What prayers did you release that seemed effective?
Whom did you turn to for wise counsel that strengthened you?

What scripture seemed to still your soul? How did you ultimately break through?

It's helpful to keep a journal during the warfare and then read through it in your debriefing. That's because you'll experience emotions and insights in the warfare that will dim after you win the battle. Many of David's psalms are somewhat like a journal entry; we see his emotions in them, for better and for worse.

If you went through a corporate battle in which others were involved, debrief as a group and learn together. Get together for coffee and discuss these same sorts of issues. In group debriefings, be sure to create a no-judgment zone so that people are free to share the intensity of their personal struggles. When you do, you'll discover that each person in the battle has valuable insights to share that will make you and others in the group stronger. Remember the goal is not to whine about how bad the warfare was, look for someone to blame, or otherwise wallow in battle wounds. If you sustained a hit during the battle that needs healing, seek healing from the Lord or from prayer warriors who went through the battle with you.

One goal of your debriefing is to learn and grow and celebrate your victory over the enemy. Another goal is to gain wisdom, understanding, and discernment. Still another goal is to position yourself to overcome faster in the next spiritual battle. Debriefing is a valuable exercise that exposes lies of the enemy you may not have recognized while you were fighting.

USE *the* DEVIL'S
MOMENTUM AGAINST HIM

I LEARNED THE PRINCIPLES of wearing out the enemy through studying mixed martial arts, especially judo. The object of judo is to throw down or take down your opponent, immobilize him, and force him to submit to your authority.

I'm spiritualizing that a bit, but that's the gist of it. The enemy wants us to submit to his authority. God wants the enemy to submit to the authority in Christ that He has given us. God expects us to enforce His will in our spheres of influence, and often that means engaging in spiritual battle. Christ won the victory. We enforce it.

Judo puts a strong focus on balance. If your enemy can get you off balance, he can throw you. First Peter 5:8–9 (AMPC) tells us to:

> Be well balanced (temperate, sober of mind), be vigilant and cautious at all times; for that enemy of yours, the devil, roams around like a lion roaring [in fierce hunger], seeking someone to seize upon and devour.
>
> Withstand him; be firm in faith [against his onset—rooted, established, strong, immovable, and determined], knowing that the same (identical) sufferings are appointed to your brotherhood (the whole body of Christians) throughout the world.

Don't let the enemy throw you off balance with his fiery darts. Don't give your mind over to thoughts of defeat, discouragement, or frustration. All these things will throw you off balance. Instead, stand in the evil day (Eph. 6:13) and know that God is able to make you stand.

In judo you use your opponent's momentum against him. At some point in your spiritual battle, the enemy will rise up and charge at you. This is when you can use spiritual momentum by moving in the opposite spirit and watch him fall.

Sometimes your enemies are unseen, but sometimes the unseen enemy works through a person. When people come against you, the carnal mind wants to strike back twice as hard, tell everyone who will listen what they did to you, and otherwise make them pay.

To stand there and take it, to give away even more than what someone is trying to force from your hands, to pray a blessing on the ones who are cursing you—that, my friends, is called moving in the opposite spirit, and in doing so you use the enemy's momentum to your benefit. Those who live a Sermon on the Mount lifestyle receive all the blessings Jesus promised in His timeless message. When you move in the opposite spirit, you avoid the bondage that the one who strikes you, sues you, takes advantage of you, gives you a hard time, or mistreats you in any way is living in. You walk free; you walk in power. And if it's a person the enemy is working through, your response might even set them free too. You overcome evil with good (Rom. 12:21). Now, you can't try to move in the opposite spirit, not really. You have to get the revelation of it and move by His grace alone. When you move in the opposite spirit of the ones who come against you, you are moving in the Holy Spirit. And you are using the enemy's momentum for his defeat and your victory. Amen.

Epilogue

A PRAYER *for*
SPIRITUAL WARRIORS

THROUGH THE PAGES of this book you've learned 101 tactics to push back darkness over your life. Now it's up to you to rise up in radical faith and put into practice what I've taught you. You can and will win every single battle you fight if you are diligent to take the Spirit-led advice and apply the scriptures outlined in this book.

I know the battle is real. I know it seems overwhelming at times. I know it's not always easy to hear from God about what to do and when to do it. Believe me, I do know. But I also know God is on your side. He will lead you even when you can't hear His voice. He will find a way to usher you into victory when you set your heart toward Him.

When you are really going through the hottest of heated fires, when the enemy has turned up the heat seven times, refer back to my prayer for you below. I am standing with you. We stand together. And the enemy is defeated.

> *Father, I thank You that You are with me and You will never leave me or forsake me, even to the end of the age. I repent of anything I've thought, said, or done that has grieved Your Spirit. If I've opened the door to the enemy, show me the door so I can shut it. If I've wronged anyone unknowingly, convict my heart so I can make it right, in Jesus's name.*
>
> *I thank You that You always lead me into triumph in Christ Jesus. God, strengthen my inner man so I can sustain this warfare. Open my eyes and help me see what is coming against me so I can fight accurately in the spirit.*

Give me Your battle plan, Your strategy, and Your tactics, in Jesus's name.

Father, help me avoid presumption. Teach my arms to bend a bow of bronze, my hands to battle, and my fingers to war. Remind me when people stand against me that my battle is not with flesh and blood. Help me to move in the opposite spirit, to bless and not curse, to walk in love, and to pray for those who persecute me. Break in with light and help me fight this battle, because my battles are Your battles. I'm merely Your battle-ax.

Rally intercessors around me to help me make it through this war. Surround me with reinforcements. Send Your angels on assignment to war on my behalf.

I take authority over every enemy attack, in the name of Jesus. I break and bind all assignments coming against my life. I stand and withstand in the evil day, wearing the full armor of God and fully equipped with the weapons of my warfare, which are not carnal but mighty through God to the pulling down of strongholds. I cast down vain imaginations and pull down every enemy stronghold over my life, in Jesus's name.

Now, Lord, I praise You for the victory. I thank You in advance that the war is won. I rejoice in You, and I am strengthened to continue fighting every good fight of faith until Your perfect will is done in my life. I give You glory and honor, for You alone are worthy of my adoration.

NOTES

Spiritual Warfare Tactic 8
BREAK WORD CURSES

1. See for example Rebecca Cecilia Yip, "The Flower Experiment," Vimeo, accessed February 5, 2018, https://vimeo.com/95391748; *Myth-Busters*, "Talking to Plants," Discovery Communications LLC, accessed November 30, 2017, http://www.discovery.com/tv-shows/mythbusters /mythbusters-database/talking-to-plants/.

Spiritual Warfare Tactic 9
CAST DOWN IMAGINATIONS

1. GreekLexicon.org, s.v. "2507: χαθαιρέω," Scripture Systems ApS, accessed February 6, 2018, http://greeklexicon.org/lexicon/strongs/2507/.
2. Blue Letter Bible, s.v. "*kathaireō*," accessed February 6, 2018, https://www.blueletterbible.org/lang/lexicon/lexicon.cfm?Strongs =G2507&t=KJV.

Spiritual Warfare Tactic 11
PUT ON YOUR BREASTPLATE OF RIGHTEOUSNESS

1. Blue Letter Bible, s.v. "*dikaiosynē*," accessed February 7, 2018, https://www.blueletterbible.org/lang/lexicon/lexicon.cfm?Strongs =G1343&t=KJV.

Spiritual Warfare Tactic 12
PUT ON YOUR HELMET OF SALVATION

1. *Merriam-Webster*, s.v. "helmet," accessed February 7, 2018, https:// www.merriam-webster.com/dictionary/helmet.
2. Blue Letter Bible, s.v. "*perikephalaia*," accessed February 7, 2018, https://www.blueletterbible.org/lang/lexicon/lexicon.cfm?Strongs =G4030&t=KJV.

3. Blue Letter Bible, s.v. "*sōtērios*," accessed February 7, 2018, https://www.blueletterbible.org/lang/lexicon/lexicon.cfm?Strongs=G4992&t=KJV.

4. Bible Hub, s.v. "*sótéria*," accessed February 7, 2018, http://biblehub.com/greek/4991.htm.

Spiritual Warfare Tactic 14
TIGHTEN YOUR BELT OF TRUTH

1. *A Few Good Men*, directed by Rob Reiner (Culver City, CA: Sony Pictures Home Entertainment, 2001), DVD.

Spiritual Warfare Tactic 17
REPENT: STRIP THE ENEMY'S RIGHTS

1. Blue Letter Bible, s.v. "*metanoeō*," accessed November 30, 2017, https://www.blueletterbible.org/lang/lexicon/lexicon.cfm?Strongs=G3340&t=KJV.

Spiritual Warfare Tactic 23
STAY FILLED WITH THE SPIRIT

1. Bill Bright, "How You Can Continue to Be Filled With the Holy Spirit," Cru, accessed February 7, 2018, https://www.cru.org/us/en/train-and-grow/10-basic-steps/3-the-holy-spirit.6.html.

Spiritual Warfare Tactic 26
MEDITATE ON THE WORD OF GOD

1. Noah Webster, *American Dictionary of the English Language* (1828), s.v. "meditate," accessed February 7, 2018, http://webstersdictionary1828.com/Dictionary/meditate.

2. Blue Letter Bible, s.v. "*hagah*," accessed February 7, 2018, https://www.blueletterbible.org/lang/lexicon/lexicon.cfm?Strongs=H1897&t=KJV.

Spiritual Warfare Tactic 27
CONFESS THE WORD OF GOD

1. Blue Letter Bible, s.v. "*homologia*," accessed February 7, 2018, https://www.blueletterbible.org/lang/lexicon/lexicon.cfm?Strongs=G3671&t=KJV; Blue Letter Bible, s.v. "*homologeō*," accessed February 7,

2018, https://www.blueletterbible.org/lang/lexicon/lexicon.cfm?strongs
=G3670&t=KJV.

2. *Merriam-Webster*, s.v. "symbiosis," accessed February 7, 2018,
https://www.merriam-webster.com/dictionary/symbiotic.

Spiritual Warfare Tactic 29
BREAK THE POWERS OF THE ENEMY

1. Blue Letter Bible, s.v. "*exousia*," accessed February 7, 2018, https://
www.blueletterbible.org/lang/lexicon/lexicon.cfm?Strongs=G1849&t
=KJV.

2. Blue Letter Bible, s.v. "*exousia*."

3. Blue Letter Bible, s.v. "*dynamis*," accessed February 7, 2018, https://
www.blueletterbible.org/lang/lexicon/lexicon.cfm?Strongs=G1411&t
=KJV.

4. Blue Letter Bible, s.v. "*adikeō*," accessed February 7, 2018, https://
www.blueletterbible.org/lang/lexicon/lexicon.cfm?Strongs=G91&t=KJV.

Spiritual Warfare Tactic 31
COME AGAINST THE ENEMY

1. Blue Letter Bible, s.v. "*pros*," accessed February 7, 2018, https://
www.blueletterbible.org/lang/lexicon/lexicon.cfm?Strongs=G4314&t
=KJV.

Spiritual Warfare Tactic 32
TAKE AUTHORITY OVER THE ENEMY

1. Blue Letter Bible, s.v. "*exousia*."

2. *Merriam-Webster*, s.v. "authority," accessed February 7, 2018,
https://www.merriam-webster.com/dictionary/authority.

3. Blue Letter Bible, s.v. "*exousia*."

4. *HELPS Word-Studies*, Bible Hub, s.v. "*exousia*," accessed February
7, 2018, http://biblehub.com/greek/1849.htm.

Spiritual Warfare Tactic 33
DON'T BREAK RANK AND ISOLATE YOURSELF

1. Christine Ammer, *The American Heritage Dictionary of Idioms*,
2nd ed. (Boston: Houghton Mifflin Harcourt, 2013), 55, https://books
.google.com/books?id=9QuEiIMaBt0C&pg.

2. Paul Heacock, ed., *Cambridge Dictionary of American Idioms* (Cambridge: Cambridge University Press, 2003), 332, https://books.google.com/books?id=ytJNRDL0zDgC&.

Spiritual Warfare Tactic 37
Ask the Holy Spirit What Weapon to Use

1. Blue Letter Bible, s.v. *"hoplon,"* accessed February 7, 2018, https://www.blueletterbible.org/lang/lexicon/lexicon.cfm?Strongs=G3696&t=KJV.
2. Blue Letter Bible, s.v. *"strateia,"* accessed February 7, 2018, https://www.blueletterbible.org/lang/lexicon/lexicon.cfm?Strongs=G4752&t=KJV.

Spiritual Warfare Tactic 39
Run to the Battle Line

1. Blue Letter Bible, s.v. *"ruwts,"* accessed February 7, 2018, https://www.blueletterbible.org/lang/lexicon/lexicon.cfm?Strongs=H7323&t=KJV.

Spiritual Warfare Tactic 40
Break Every Yoke

1. *Merriam-Webster,* s.v. "yoke," accessed February 7, 2018, https://www.merriam-webster.com/dictionary/yoke.

Spiritual Warfare Tactic 41
Break the Stranglehold of Worry

1. *Merriam-Webster,* s.v. "stranglehold," accessed February 8, 2018, https://www.merriam-webster.com/dictionary/stranglehold.
2. *Merriam-Webster,* s.v. "worry," accessed February 8, 2018, https://www.merriam-webster.com/dictionary/worry.

Spiritual Warfare Tactic 42
Break Deception Off Your Mind

1. Walter Kambulow, *Blessed to Be a Blessing* (Burlington, Ontario: Victory Ministries, 2009), 67, https://books.google.com/books?id=xswpOuv7p2MC&pg.

Spiritual Warfare Tactic 43
CALL YOUR INTERCESSORS

1. C. Peter Wagner, *Prayer Shield* (Ventura, CA: Regal Books, 1992).

Spiritual Warfare Tactic 49
RESIST THE DEVIL

1. Bible Hub, s.v. *"anthistémi,"* accessed February 8, 2018, http://biblehub.com/greek/436.htm.

Spiritual Warfare Tactic 53
RENEW YOUR MIND IN THE AREA OF ATTACK

1. Blue Letter Bible, s.v. *"anakainōsis,"* accessed February 9, 2018, https://www.blueletterbible.org/lang/lexicon/lexicon.cfm?Strongs=G342&t=KJV.

Spiritual Warfare Tactic 55
REFUSE TO FOLLOW YOUR EMOTIONS

1. Watchman Nee, *The Spiritual Man* (Bon Air, VA: Christian Fellowship Publishers, 2009), https://books.google.com/books?id=DcpOBAAAQBAJ&pg.

Spiritual Warfare Tactic 60
SHUT YOUR EARS TO THE ACCUSER OF THE BRETHREN

1. *Merriam-Webster,* s.v. "slander," accessed February 13, 2018, https://www.merriam-webster.com/dictionary/slander.

Spiritual Warfare Tactic 64
STOP WHINING ABOUT THE WARFARE

1. Blue Letter Bible, s.v. *"goggyzō,"* accessed February 13, 2018, https://www.blueletterbible.org/lang/lexicon/lexicon.cfm?Strongs=G1111&t=KJV.

Spiritual Warfare Tactic 65
REJOICE IN THE LORD

1. Rick Renner, "The Apostle Paul and His Letter to the Church at Philippi ~ [Book of Philippians]" (sermon, Tulsa, OK, March 12, 1997), http://pastornolan.blogspot.com/2012/04/apostale-paul-and-his-letter-to-church.html.

Spiritual Warfare Tactic 66
Push Back the Darkness

1. Blue Letter Bible, s.v. "kosmokratōr," accessed February 13, 2018, https://www.blueletterbible.org/lang/lexicon/lexicon.cfm?Strongs =G2888&t=KJV.

2. Blue Letter Bible, s.v. "skotos," accessed February 9, 2018, https:// www.blueletterbible.org/lang/lexicon/lexicon.cfm?Strongs=G4655&t =KJV.

3. Joseph S. Exell and Henry Donald Maurice Spence-Jones, "Commentary on Ephesians 6:12," *The Pulpit Commentary* (1897), https:// www.studylight.org/commentaries/tpc/ephesians-6.html.

Spiritual Warfare Tactic 67
Withstand Weariness

1. *Merriam-Webster*, s.v. "weary," accessed February 13, 2018, https:// www.merriam-webster.com/dictionary/weary.

Spiritual Warfare Tactic 70
Close the Door on Strife

1. *Merriam-Webster*, s.v. "strife," accessed February 13, 2018, https:// www.merriam-webster.com/dictionary/strife.

Spiritual Warfare Tactic 75
Reject Presumption and Assumption in the Battle

1. *Merriam-Webster*, s.v. "presume," accessed February 15, 2018, http://www.wordcentral.com/cgi-bin/thesaurus?book=Thesaurus&va =presume.

2. *Merriam-Webster*, s.v. "presumptuous," accessed February 15, 2018, https://www.merriam-webster.com/dictionary/presumptuous.

3. *Merriam-Webster*, s.v. "assume," accessed February 15, 2018, https://www.merriam-webster.com/dictionary/assume.

4. *Merriam-Webster*, s.v. "insolent," accessed February 15, 2018, https://www.merriam-webster.com/dictionary/insolent.

5. *Merriam-Webster*, s.v. "audacity," accessed February 15, 2018, https://www.merriam-webster.com/dictionary/audacity.

6. Blue Letter Bible, s.v. "zuwd," accessed February 15, 2018, https:// www.blueletterbible.org/lang/lexicon/lexicon.cfm?Strongs=H2102&t =KJV; Blue Letter Bible, s.v. "zed," accessed February 9, 2018, https:// www.blueletterbible.org/lang/lexicon/lexicon.cfm?Strongs=H2086&t

=KJV; Blue Letter Bible, s.v. "*tolmētēs*," accessed February 15, 2018, https://www.blueletterbible.org/lang/lexicon/lexicon.cfm?Strongs =G5113&t=KJV.

Spiritual Warfare Tactic 82
Act Like the Persistent Widow

1. W. E. Vine, *Vine's Expository Dictionary of New Testament Words*, s.v. "knock," StudyLight.org, accessed February 15, 2018, https://www .studylight.org/dictionaries/ved/k/knock.html.

Spiritual Warfare Tactic 86
Surrender Everything to God

1. *Merriam-Webster*, s.v. "surrender," accessed February 15, 2018, https://www.merriam-webster.com/dictionary/surrender.

Spiritual Warfare Tactic 92
Discern Spiritual Climates

1. *Merriam-Webster*, s.v. "climate," accessed February 15, 2018, https://www.merriam-webster.com/dictionary/climate.

Spiritual Warfare Tactic 94
Bind the Strongman

1. Blue Letter Bible, s.v. "*ischyros*," accessed February 15, 2018, https://www.blueletterbible.org/lang/lexicon/lexicon.cfm?Strongs =G2478&t=KJV.

2. "'Spoilers' in the Bible," Knowing-Jesus.com, accessed February 15, 2018, https://bible.knowing-jesus.com/words/Spoilers.

3. *Merriam-Webster*, s.v. "plunder," accessed February 15, 2018, https://www.merriam-webster.com/dictionary/plunder.

Spiritual Warfare Tactic 96
Overcome Demonic Overwhelm

1. *Merriam-Webster*, s.v. "overwhelm," accessed February 15, 2018, https://www.merriam-webster.com/dictionary/overwhelm.

Spiritual Warfare Tactic 97
BREAK THOUGHT CURSES

1. Blue Letter Bible, s.v. *"qalal,"* accessed February 15, 2018, https://www.blueletterbible.org/lang/lexicon/lexicon.cfm?Strongs=H7043&t=KJV.

Spiritual Warfare Tactic 99
DON'T UNDERESTIMATE YOUR ENEMY

1. Billy Graham, *The Journey* (Nashville, TN: Thomas Nelson, 2006), 35, https://books.google.com/books?id=1JEUFIv_Br4C&pg.

Spiritual Warfare Tactic 100
DEBRIEF AFTER THE BATTLE

1. *Merriam-Webster,* s.v. "debrief," accessed February 15, 2018, https://www.merriam-webster.com/dictionary/debrief.